HOW SCHOOLS MIGHT BE GOVERNED AND WHY

SEYMOUR B. SARASON

Teachers College, Columbia University
New York and London

Published by Teachers College Press, 1234 Amsterdam Avenue, New York, N.Y. 10027

Library of Congress Cataloging-in-Publication Data
Sarason, Seymour Bernard, 1919-
How schools might be governed and why / Seymour B. Sarason.
　　p.　cm.
Includes bibliographical references (p.　) and index.
ISBN 0-8077-3642-2 (cloth : alk. paper). — ISBN 0-8077-3641-4 (pbk. : alk. paper)
1. School management and organization—United States. 2. Educational change—United States. I. Title.
LB2805.S2668 1997
371.2'00973—dc21　　　　　　　　　　　　97-1456

ISBN 0-8077-3641-4 (paper)
ISBN 0-8077-3642-2 (cloth)

Printed on acid-free paper
Manufactured in the United States of America
04 03 02 01 00 99 98 97　　8 7 6 5 4 3 2 1

How Schools Might Be Governed and Why

*To Irma Süsskeit Miller
with my love*

Contents

PREFACE

I had to overcome a number of obstacles, personal and substantive, to get to the point where I could begin to write this book. I say personal because I knew that what I wanted to say would be, had to be, indeed should be, incomplete given its subject matter. No individual should be expected to have that degree of knowledge, experience, imagination, and creativity to come up with a plan for a new system of educational governance in which all problems have been identified and secure answers are clearly provided. Our educational system is comprised of more than schools or school systems. The legislative and executive branches of local, state, and federal government are parts of the system, as are the state department of education, colleges and universities, and parents. However these parts are coordinated, and they are very poorly coordinated, it is a complex system. If you were to believe the organizational chart depicting the system, the parts are clear in their role and purpose and in the ways they relate to and support each other. As is usually the case with organizational charts, in the "real" world the picture is very different. That is the case with our educational system, and it is also the case with any large public or private organization, which is why I and Elizabeth Lorentz wrote a book with the title *Coordination: Process, Problems, and Opportunities. In Schools, Private Sector, and Federal Government.*

The governance of the educational system probably can be described by one person, although if that person sought to distinguish between what the system appears to be and the myriad of ways that appearance is belied in practice, I doubt that one person could do justice to that goal. If you have come to conclude, as I have, that the existing governance system is very inadequate and unrescuable and you wish to start from scratch with a new system, you have to be possessed of a significant degree of grandiosity to assume that one person can think through the ins and the outs of the posed problem as well as of the plan he or she comes up with. It is a task for a group of people, each of whom is a critical sounding board for others, each of whom varies in degree and kinds of relevant experience, and all of whom willingly acknowledge that the task they have taken on requires a sustained, difficult group effort. The best model in human history is the constitutional convention of 1787, which was in near daily session for several months in Philadelphia. They did not (initially) seek to repair the dangerously inadequate Articles of Confederation. They started from scratch, so to speak. No one of them, no small fraction of them, could have come up with what the larger convention ultimately produced. In several of my books I have pleaded for such a convention on the governance of our educational system. As I expected, the response has been total silence, even though I have never met an educator, a foundation executive, or anyone in the Department of Education in Washington who answered the following question in the affirmative: If you were starting from scratch, would you come up with the present system of governance? When I would ask what alternative they would propose, it was obvious that they had never truly tried to outline an alternative. As one person said, "Why waste time fantasizing? What we have is locked in concrete and unlike the Berlin Wall it will not come down." I sympathized with her stance because I had felt the same way.

There was another obstacle. Any system of governance has a purpose which that system is expressly obligated to achieve. There may be more than one purpose, but there is always one overarching purpose, i.e., a purpose judged so important that when it is not achieved, all other purposes stand little chance of being achieved. Is there such an overarching purpose informing and powering the governance of education? On the level of rhetoric there is such a purpose, and it is usually put in this way: "To help each child realize his or her potential." I am by no means alone in regarding that statement as empty rhetoric violated every day in almost all classrooms in almost all schools. Our current system of educational governance has not in the past or in the present reflected that purpose, and it cannot reflect it in the future. Indeed, the system is not for that purpose but against it. That, I hasten to add, has not been "willed" by anyone or any group. There are no villains in that sense. That meant to me that the initial step in the task is not to come up with a plan but with a clear statement of a rationale justifying governance because if there is no clarity or agreement about rationale, the plan you come up with is doomed. I felt secure about what I considered a clear statement of purpose just as I was secure that the current form of government was a very large part of the problem and in no way could be part of the solution.

So what governance system could I propose that stood a good chance of doing justice to the overarching purpose? When I started to try to answer that question, I confess that I was overwhelmed by the number of practical details any comprehensive scheme would encounter. At some point I found myself asking this question: How did we get to the point of putting humans into outer space? A more instructive form of the question became: Early in this century when the science and engineering of rocketry developed, what did those pioneers know, what more did they know they would have to learn, in order for humans to be sent into space and to return *safely*. The overarching purpose was to demonstrate that human space flight was possible but *not* at the cost of human life. As time went on and accumulating knowledge and experience (some of it tragic) indicated that putting humans into outer space was not the stuff of dreams, the safety issue became more salient and very complex. In brief, whatever system of flight was developed it had to meet the most stringent criteria for safety. Knowing as they did that the developing system would encounter predictable and unpredictable problems, that system had to be a self-correcting one, i.e., a system that at all stages of development had to be one of continuous improvement.

I realized that although I was clear about the overarching purpose a governance system of education must serve, I should not expect that I would be able to do other than to be concrete about some of the features of a new system. Knowing that I would leave many questions unanswered—legitimate, practical questions—I put writing the book aside. Frankly, I was intimidated by visions of readers saying, "What about this problem? What about that problem? You are giving us nothing like a blueprint by which to judge whether what you are giving us is another example of problem creation through problem solution. That is to say, the cure is no better, and perhaps worse, than the disease." And, yet, I could not let go of my belief that the fate of our educational system, and that of our society, required a new system of governance. Was it not my obligation to what I believed to do the best I could about where, why, and how we should begin even though I would leave many questions unanswered?

I do not say this as an excuse for what I have written but as explanation. At the very least, it is my hope that what I have written will stimulate other individuals and groups to deal forthrightly with the governance issue. If you believe that the current system of governance is rescuable, you are likely to react negatively to what I have to say. If you believe it is not rescuable and seek a blueprint for action, you will conclude that I have fallen far short of the mark. But if you believe it is not rescuable and you are open to consider a sketch for a new vision, what I have written may be of interest to you. Each of us has been brought up in the current educational system.

We take it for granted even though, I have to repeat, no knowledgeable person will say that if he or she started from scratch, they would reinvent what we now have.

History will render its verdict about how we dealt with an educational system the inadequacies and failures of which started to become obvious as soon as World War II ended and with each passing year became a source of societal bewilderment because whatever remedial measures were taken, requiring the expenditure of scores of billions of dollars, the system seemed intractable to change. In 1971 I wrote *The Culture of the School and the Problem of Change*. In 1996 I was asked to add to that book how things have changed in the quarter of a century since the first edition. That book was titled *Revisiting the Culture of the School and the Problem of Change*. Among the changes I discuss one is most relevant here: Whereas 25 years ago many people, within and outside the educational community, believed that increasing expenditures would improve educational outcomes, there are very few people who hold that belief today. Indeed, most people today, again within and outside the educational community, are truly puzzled about how the system and its outcomes can be generally improved. In an inchoate way they know that working within the present system is an exercise in futility.

I can assure the reader that I know that I have not cornered the market on truth and wisdom. What I do have are some strong convictions about what is wrong and the direction we should go. It took me decades to arrive at those convictions, to see the system for what I think it is. Having arrived at those convictions, I felt obliged to present them to those with a vital interest in our schools.

Some readers may be critical of what they perceive to be an unjustified criticism of all educators, and an unwarranted derogation or ignoring of what some teachers in some schools are doing in line with the overarching purpose of education. As I have said many times in the past, and reiterate in this book, I know from personal experience that there are such teachers and classrooms. Not only are their numbers few but in every instance I have observed the school and school system literally did nothing to seek to spread the message and practice. The governance system is simply and blatantly not geared to learn and to spread that learning. And, I must add, in a fair number of these instances what these teachers were doing was despite and not because of the system of governance. And what I just said is no less true for principals. This book is not about the personalities and abilities of educators but about a system that is as stultifying for teachers and principals as it is for students. As I shall emphasize in this book, *when contexts of productive learning do not exist for teachers, they cannot create and sustain that kind of context for students.* For those readers who, having read this preface, decide to read no further, I suggest they see the movie *Mr. Holland's Opus*. It is the best visual depiction of the major themes contained in the pages that follow.

Words are inadequate to express my gratitude to and affection for Lisa Pagliaro whose graciousness, geniality, and good humor are matched only by her mind-boggling capacity to make sense of my handwriting.

How schools might be governed and why

C H A P T E R

Statement of the Problem

There is more than one way to approach and state a problem, and any such statement has more than one source. Aside from reading and observation, I have been mightily influenced by talking to people in what I shall call the "trenches," i.e., in their daily lives they *have* to grapple with problems in which I, not in the trenches, am interested. That is why I begin the book with interviews that contain themes that I will discuss in later chapters. These interviews are kin to the overture to an opera or musical: They contain the major themes, at least most of them. They are not essential to my argument, but they represent the kinds of "talking data" that were essential to the development of my point of view.

VIEW A

Professors Sidney Trubowitz and Paul Longo currently work for the Center for the Improvement of Education at Queens College in New York City. Beginning in 1979 they spearheaded a collaboration between the new Louis Armstrong Middle School (I.S. 227) and a group of Queen's faculty. After 5 years they published a book *When a College and a School Work Together* (1984). After 17 years of the collaboration they wrote a follow-up book, *How It Works: Inside a School/College Collaboration* (1997). I was a consultant to the collaboration during the first 5 years. Since then the three of us have met several times a year in New Haven to discuss "how things are going." What follows is my distillation of our conversations. Professors Trubowitz and Longo read what follows, and I am grateful both for their stamp of approval and permission to use the "interview" here.

SBS: Before becoming faculty members at Queens both of you were classroom teachers and then administrators. As you know, I am especially interested in how schools and school systems are governed and how that governance is experienced and reacted to by teachers, principals, etc. What were your experiences when you were on the front line?

ST: That is a tall order because your question elicits a cascade of memories that is not easy to categorize. Let me start with a caveat: How anyone in the front line answers that question is in large measure a function of the kind of person he or she is.

PL: It also depends on how long the person has been in the system. A new teacher or principal would not answer it in the same way as someone who has been in the system for, let us say, 5 or more years.

SBS: You are both right, of course, so let me ask this question: How did you experience the school in your early years as a teacher?

ST: I had a sense of strangeness and loneliness. It seemed as if I was surrounded by people who apparently knew what they were doing. I felt totally otherwise. I floundered, pushed ahead, tried to do the best I could. Other teachers were kind to me but they had little time to give help. My principal was some distant figure who was preoccupied with many other things rather than how I was doing in the classroom.

SBS: Was your principal informative or supportive?

ST: I don't remember him as either. Periodically, he would come to my class to do a formal observation, and we'd have a brief conversation afterwards. He would also funnel directives to the total staff from the central administration. The directives were largely about what we could or should not do. I would have trouble dredging up instances where the directives encouraged us to do this or that. For the most part he seemed bogged down in other things— parents, the community, the district office—and had little time to give attention to day-to-day teaching.

SBS: How do you think the principal reacted to the directives?

PL: Most come to see these as defining areas of primary concern. My first principal had been in the role for many years. She was a very nice person who tried to run an efficient school. That efficiency did not extend to a deep interest in the actual activity conducted in the classroom. If there were no parent complaints, it was generally assumed all was going well. It was not that she lacked a sincere interest in education, it was just that she saw little or no need for making significant changes. Her notion of a good school was characterized by quiet children, parents with few or no complaints, and teachers who did not bring her their problems. She did not recognize that one could meet these goals and there was still much more that could be done.

ST: Paul is making an important point. My principal like others let the teachers know that he regarded the system as something from which you maintain distance and which you try to keep under control. Within broad limits he did what he thought was right and did not much care if it departed from standard operating procedures. His aim always was to maneuver the system for the benefit of the school.

SBS: You considered him supportive?

ST: He was reasonably supportive. Mostly he left me alone. And I was alone, and I mean *alone*. You dealt with your anxieties and confusion on your own. For me, as for most teachers, getting through the first year was a definite challenge. The other teachers were friendly, but they did not offer much help. The teaching culture, then and now, treats performance in the classroom as an individual activity. You are expected to learn and handle most of your responsibilities on your own. You might say that I spent my first year trying to overcome my lack of knowledge and experience.

PL: I believe that pattern is true for most beginning teachers. It is often sink or swim. Most learn to swim, but you have to accomplish it pretty much on your own. There are no lifeguards, no strong support system. One of the great drawbacks of this approach, what Sid and I call the Darwinian induction model, is that you can learn some very bad teaching habits.

SBS: But you did survive. Both of you more than survived.

PL: I guess we did.

SBS: Then the system could not have been all bad.

PL: Sid and I have discussed that many times. We did not survive because of the structure or any system of support. Most of the teachers I knew were seeking to function in ways that made for the least disruption, to make life in the schools as painless as possible. The vast majority were not lacking in ability, but they were not being challenged to grow. They did their jobs quietly, without fuss, but often without experiencing the satisfactions (and frustrations) that come with trying something new. The rewards, the approbation, came from creating stable environments and not from taking risks.

SBS: So how come you were different? What helped you to move forward? Were you better prepared in your training?

ST: No, not necessarily. We have read what you have written about teacher preparation programs. Someplace in one of your books you say about such programs that you judge them the way musicians judge a Beethoven violin concerto: It's not for the violin but against it. We can agree with some of the inner meaning of that comparison. We were generally not prepared for the realities of school and school systems. Over the years, however, we have both come to believe that you cannot learn some of the critical aspects of the role in preparatory programs. Some things you will only learn when you get your own classroom and so you need good first-year support systems for new teachers.

SBS: Still, you did more than survive. Both of you sought to and did expand your knowledge. You were readers. You feared succumbing to the system. You wanted to better reach and stimulate your students. You wanted to institute certain changes. You did not want to be doing next year what you were doing this year. You needed to feel you were growing, not standing still. I am not saying you were paragons of perfection. Both of you knew that your choice was between developing or looking elsewhere for satisfaction. And I have come to know the both of you well enough to say that underneath your mild, very friendly exteriors are a lot of self-confidence and personal–intellectual ambition.

PL: I don't think we would quarrel with the part about wanting to grow and change. But, to be honest, I think you may be underestimating the number of new teachers who, like us, wanted to make improvements in their settings but were in schools that offered little support and they ended up retreating into themselves. What you need to keep in mind is that in New York, as in many urban areas, new teachers tend to be put in the most difficult schools. That is where the greatest turnover occurs and where the largest number of placements are made. It was true years ago, and it is not much different today. I think Sid will agree that there are increasing numbers of new teachers who leave teaching within the first 2 years. One can understand that the City is not anxious to publicize such figures, but we have heard that they range as high as 70%.

ST: In some ways it was different when I began as a teacher. I think conditions were less harsh. What is the same is the problem of isolation, aloneness. I needed more. I needed the sense that there were others with whom you could share ideas. I needed to believe that thinking and exploring were part of the job.

SBS: Let's skip years now and turn to the I.S. 227 (Louis Armstrong Middle School)–Queens College collaboration. How did you get involved in that?

ST: Saul Cohen became president of the college and, unlike most who get to this position, he was seriously interested in public education. He knew the new chancellor of the school system, and he worked out a deal whereby a relatively small cadre of the education faculty would commit a large part of their time to participating in the development of I.S. 227. The school had been built but was never opened because of a court order preventing its use before a plan was presented insuring that it would be a 55/45 integrated school. In typical Saul Cohen style he asked me along with John Lidstone to get a few other faculty members to figure out how we could be helpful, how we could forge a relationship that would contribute both to I.S. 227 and the school of education. I say "typical Saul Cohen style" because he left it up to us to do it our way, with the assurance that we had his support. We were not used to a president who felt so keenly that the college had a responsibility to the public schools. And we were not used to a president who acted on that sense of responsibility, who was eager and willing to use college resources of many kinds to make that possible. Saul was a master at cutting red tape or even trampling on it. So, if we are going to talk about the collaboration, it will have to be divided into two parts: the 5 years he was president and what came after.

PL: There was another crucial person and that was the dean of the school of education, John Lidstone. Not only was he supportive, but he actively participated in our planning meetings, and he was a familiar face at I.S. 227. He retired soon after Saul Cohen resigned to spend more time on his research and writing. The timing of John's retirement was not fortuitous. The president who followed Saul Cohen did not share his deep interest in the state of pre-college education. Our presence in the school was viewed as useful, but that interest did not match the level of psychological and material support Saul Cohen provided. Support diminished at other levels as well. We were left increasingly on our own. In a certain sense this paralleled our early experience as teachers. You grow to learn that most efforts in the field of education are highly isolated or compartmentalized and that we have tended to institutionalize this isolation. For example, we have created the myth of the good teacher as a loner. I recently came across a comment by Ann Cook, a New York City principal, that makes the point nicely. She complains about the way our popular media present the good teacher as a rebel or iconoclast. She is bothered by this portrayal of successful teachers as people who heroically defy rather than define the institutions in which they work. Her view is that it takes a whole community to educate a child, that putting our hopes in isolated individuals is a dead end.

ST: Returning to John Lidstone for a moment: Paul is absolutely right about his importance. After John and Saul left the scene, the ball game changed. The type of school–college collaboration that is developed depends, to an important degree, on how well the top administrative layers of each of the partners knows about and supports what is going on. And when I say "know" I mean they want to know, they are interested in how things are going. After Saul and John left we realized that aside from a handful of us at the college, few are vitally interested. From that point on we were left to deal on our own with layers of the school system that had little interest in the collaboration. From one year to the next we did not know if the policy makers downtown would withdraw their support. We felt the way many classroom teachers do: Where is the interest in what we are trying to do?

SBS: Can you be more specific about the content of those struggles?

PL: Let's begin by giving you some objective facts. The collaboration is in its 17th year. During that time we have had eight chancellors of the New York City public school system. At I.S. 227 we have had seven principals and a number of different assistant principals. Fortunately, and I think this says a lot, teacher turnover has been well below the average of the New York City school system. Now, when any of those in key areas of responsibility left, we felt a distinct void. That is true of any school trying to organize itself in an unusual way. I.S. 227 had a distinctive program and culture that required a degree of collegiality demanded by few schools in the system. There are 1,400 students, the school is racially integrated, parents play a very important role, the school day is longer than that of most schools, and there are large numbers of other adults present besides the school staff. In terms of results, pupil achievement is high, there is no graffiti on the wall inside the school, teachers want to remain there, we have had few racial incidents, and parents, community people, and other visitors come and go with high frequency. All this did not come about by a random process. It took time and the energy of everyone, far beyond what is usually the case. So, when a principal leaves—usually to a higher administrative position and salary—it makes a difference who the replacement will be. The manner in which such choices are made is part chance, part arbitrary bureaucratic decision making. The particular needs of this specific culture are not a primary factor.

SBS: So there were occasions when a new administrator came in as an unknown quantity.

ST: Right. And each time we and the school staff had to adjust to a new personality, to their different sense of the collaboration, their limited knowledge of the school's prior history of its culture, and a new agenda, since each person brought his or her own ideas of what a middle school should be.

SBS: In light of the fact that you are still there, you seemed to have made successful accommodation to the new people.

ST: For the most part, yes. The vast majority had never been in a school where there is as close and as extensive a collaboration between a school and a college. That required a lot of adjustment on their part. Some were comfortable sharing ideas and collaborating on direction. Some were not. Most came with their own views about what they wanted to do and accomplish. They didn't seek the position to conform to the way things were; they had their own educational theory and agenda. Our role required us to make appropriate adjustments. It was our goal not to clash or exert pressure. Remember, from the time the collaboration started, we made it explicit that we were not there to tell anybody what to do. We were there to discuss and exchange ideas, to be helpful in mutually rewarding ways. We were lucky in that the first principal was a person who loved to exchange ideas. With several of the principals you could put anything on the table and not worry that it would be misinterpreted or turned into a personal disagreement. We appreciated them, and they appreciated us. In fact, we were frequently sought out and conferred with about procedures. Others were not always as accessible or open to the sharing of different ideas.

PL: Sid and I have talked a lot about this and we agreed that over time, it is more and more difficult to maintain an effective collaboration. The more distant you are from the passion and commitment that initially propelled the endeavor, the more difficult it is to maintain momentum. The original version is no longer shared, and there has not been adequate time to meet with the new leadership and develop alternatives that might similarly fire the professional imagination of the staff.

SBS: Did any of the principals go to bat for you at the central office?

PL: Yes. Some did. There were several school administrators who did not meekly accede to the typical bureaucratic restrictions that inhibit the possibility of change in the schools. We can't say that for all of them, but there were several. As I noted, however, the support tends to diminish over time. That was also true at the college. After Saul Cohen there was no one at that level who was similarly interested in what we were doing. Interest remained, but not active support, and that makes a world of difference.

SBS: So what incentives were there for you to persist?

ST: Our relationship with and support from teachers and parents. There was also the fact that we believed something important was being done. We were still discussing and trying new ideas. There are always times when you need to give serious thought to whether there are sufficient advantages to continuing. Up to this point the answer has been yes, but that is always subject to change. Our first book was written 5 years after we started. We would never have thought at the time that we would be writing another one after 12 more years of continuous collaboration. The longer we have been there, the more we have had to conclude that school change requires people who are carefully chosen and provided with special support if the built-in deficits of the system are to be overcome.

PL: There's another factor that needs emphasis. The fact is that the central office knew little about the collaboration. Periodically, we were obliged to give a report describing the inception of the collaboration, how it worked, and other details to people who had never before heard about it. The point was that no one at the central office knew anything about I.S. 227 except that it received this or that national award. They rarely visited the school. On the other hand, Saul Cohen and John Lidstone came to the school a number of times. John was a frequent visitor, and he and Clarence Bunch helped Anthony San Fillipo, the school's first principal, to see the educational benefits to be derived by creating an art gallery out of a regular classroom. We are especially proud of that gallery, and so is everyone in the school. After Saul and John left, there were fewer visits to the school from people at this level.

SBS: Given the local and national recognition the school received, is it strange that central office did not give much attention as to how to apply what was done and what was learned to other middle schools?

ST: No, it's not strange. A few years ago when the contract between the college and the school came up for renewal, we were asked to meet with the central administrative office. The Chancellor's representatives suggested to us that they were working on a proposal to make the contract renewable on a yearly basis and putting it out for bid to other colleges or universities. Now that betrays a serious misunderstanding of what school/college collaboration is all about. It didn't happen, but that they thought you could bring in a new group of people every year demonstrates a poor grasp of reality, let alone a collaborative endeavor. On another occasion, at the time of contract renewal, it was suggested that we maintain Louis Armstrong as a base, but shift the bulk of our effort to schools the city had identified as "failing." No one was suggesting significant changes in how the schools were run or who was running them. The view seemed to be that we could be sent in, uninvited by the school staff, to work with them on this external perception of their failures. There was no discussion of what additional resources would be necessary to take on another school, of how I.S. 227 could be used as a kind of training institute, or of any possible ways in which the collaboration's experience at 227 could be utilized. No, the proposal was to move to another school and try to turn things around, following which we would move to another school.

SBS: I want you to elaborate on that, but there is a question I have been meaning to ask. The question is this: Each year the powers that be have to decide whether they want to continue the collaboration. The college contributes resources in terms of time, tuition, and a lot of graduate interns. The system pays the college an amount of money that the college uses to fund your activity. On what basis does the system decide to say yes or no about continuation? What formal evaluation do they base their decision on?

ST: Let Paul answer that. He has had a lot of experience with evaluations done by the school system.

PL: There are two parts to the answer. Only one formal evaluation
        was done, and it happened early in the life of the collaboration. It
        was a favorable evaluation based on visits to the school, some
        analysis of student achievement, and interviews of school and col-
        lege staff. It certainly was not an in-depth or comprehensive one.
        The second part of the answer is that the evaluation was done not
        because there was any burning desire to have one but rather
        because rules and regulations say an evaluation must be done. In
        our case, as is generally true, evaluation was neither planned nor
        were budgetary resources provided. The general view was that you
        could conduct the evaluation out of the operational budget. Just
        ask a few key questions. But evaluation is not a matter of sampling
        opinion, asking people, "How do you think things are going? Are
        your goals being achieved?" The problems is that this limited per-
        spective is not peculiar to New York City. It's true of every school
        system I've ever known. That's why we learn so little from reform
        or change efforts. We do not know if and why an effort succeeded
        or failed. Evaluation is a form of research—at the very least it
        should be—but you will never find the word *research* as a line
        item in the budget of a school system. That is probably the case
        for the word *evaluation*. Research is looked upon as a frill, some-
        thing academics do.

SBS: I did not intend to ask about this, Sid, but you spent some time
        directing a large collaborative effort in a suburban environment.
        What are the one or two major differences you saw between New
        York City and suburban schools?

ST: I have thought about that but not in any systematic way. One
        thing I am sure of: the differences are one of degree. In the
        smaller suburban communities of high economic status, there are
        more likely to be parents accustomed to raising questions about
        how their child is faring and being handled. These parents have no
        compunctions, if they don't get their way, of making a fuss at
        school board meetings. Superintendents in these communities, like
        superintendents elsewhere, are not anxious to have open conflict.
        In these wealthy communities parents who are dissatisfied will be
        quick to bring about a debate on this or that teacher, principal, or
        practice. And so it is that superintendents in these affluent districts
        are especially sensitive to parental opinion and criticism. Although
        superintendents will say favorable things about parental involve-
        ment, the aim most often is to avoid intrusion into what are con-
        sidered professional matters.

SBS: You used the adjective nonintrusive two or three times. Am I wrong in saying that in their public statements these superintendents will say favorable things about parental involvement?

ST: You are right.

PL: What Sid has said applies to communities in New York City as well. There are neighborhoods, affluent and otherwise, that exist in the city where parents are quite prepared to question and resist educational approaches if they feel they depart from their own views of what schools should be doing. Look what happened with regard to ex-Chancellor Fernandez and the Rainbow Curriculum. If parents feel they are not getting the hearing they believe they deserve and they go to the district superintendent's office, you can bet they are going to be listened to seriously and some action will be taken. What we tried to do at I.S. 227 from the beginning was create a forum and an atmosphere where parents could bring up what was on their minds or in their interest. For the most part, schools are not interested in doing this. There are dangers, and their reticence is understandable. Still, it is like trying to sit on a three-legged stool with one leg missing.

SBS: Let's return to something we were discussing earlier. You said that a couple of years ago the central office wanted you to shift your efforts to other middle schools that were in trouble. How did you handle the situation?

PL: As I noted earlier, we told them we could not work with other schools unless a supportive climate could be created. Change cannot be accomplished without a clear commitment on the part of the school community, not only its leadership. I am fascinated with the preliminary report done on the Coalition of Essential Schools. The reviewers noted that several of the schools that enthusiastically joined the coalition did so without feeling there would be any need for them to make any change in the way they were operating. I find that instructive. The belief that we can make progress without making any substantial change is widespread. In any event, our discussion with central administration about moving on to new schools turned out to be a short one. We were never able to get into a conversation about what was needed to effect change in troubled schools.

SBS: There is nothing gratifying about that type of exchange.

PL: The gratifying part is what the parents at I.S. 227 did. They let downtown know that they would take our leaving seriously. We figured that when the parents heard about the possibility of the collaboration ending, they would be upset. The college had been an integral part of the school for so long. We anticipated they would communicate their dissatisfaction, but frankly we did not expect they would act as directly, clearly, and as strongly as they did. And the same happened with teachers. That was immensely encouraging. These are two groups whose support meant a great deal to us. They, more than almost any other part of the system, placed real value on what we were doing.

SBS: So the Board decided to renew the contract for the collaboration?

PL: Yes. We continue on a short-term basis, but I have no doubt the battle will be resumed. That's school life. For all we know the next principal may not be disposed to conducting a collaborative effort or will support it in name only.

ST: But whatever happens we've learned how important parents can be. We've seen by the questions they ask how they keep a school thinking about what it's doing. We've also found out that parents are your strongest allies when political clout is needed to stop arbitrary actions by the central bureaucracy. We have tried to listen to them and to treat their ideas with respect. The result, from our vantage point, has been strong support for many of the positive endeavors that have been attempted.

SBS: Did you let officialdom at the college know about the possibility of the project folding?

PL: Yes. It is part of our role to keep them informed, but I don't think it has been a cause of deep concern. The involvement of the college with public schools has been seen as a project, an extra endeavor, not something that is important to the overall mission. Saul Cohen once said that colleges need to cease behaving as if their freshmen are delivered to campus by a stork and not a school system. He was implying, of course, that we have an unacknowledged partnership and it would be wise to extend a helping hand. It is good advice, but it has been largely ignored.

VIEW B

Saul Cohen is an old friend and colleague. Few people have been involved in diverse aspects of public education more than he has, despite the fact that his formal training (and long experience as a researcher) was not as an educator. As in view A, the following is a distillation of countless discussions in a wide assortment of venues. I am once again grateful for permission to use this material.

SBS: In the heyday of the sixties when the Office of Education was funding school change efforts by the dozens, you were not only involved in several of them but you helped formulate them. How come?

SC: The key person for me in the Office of Education was a historian, Don Bigelow, whom I had known previously. My interests were several. First, how to get more minorities interested in a career as a professional geographer. In this case, Don took over the support of a program that I had initiated through the National Science Foundation (NSF). Second, to get teachers of teachers to understand that geography was more, much more, than making maps or getting students to know how to locate a country on a map. Geography has become connected with some of the physical sciences and with the social sciences as well, and, I must add, with matters of health and disease. While I had been active in developing geography curriculum programs for both high school and college supported by the NSF, it was Don who involved me in NDEA Training Institute for Teachers. Third, it was self-evident to me that colleges and universities could and should not be as unrelated to the public schools as they were. It was also Don Bigelow who was primarily responsible for initiating The Teachers of Teachers (TTT) program, which was broad in scope and well-funded, and it was Don who supported the efforts of Paul Ward the historian and myself to create the Consortium of Professional Associations for the Teaching of the Social Sciences. So, it was through Don that I could pursue my interests.

SBS: And it was through you that I got to know Don, who is quite a character.

SC: An understatement. What was truly distinctive about Don was that he was a highly trained, far more than competent professional historian who was vitally interested in improving the public schools. Before coming to the Office of Education he taught at Columbia. It may be the case that he gave the first for-credit history course on public television, usually given at an ungodly morning hour. Don was always interested in teaching, and he had a social conscience. So he jumped at the chance to give his all to improving schools by upgrading teachers' knowledge of subject matter.

SBS: Don was a passionate advocate for the liberal arts. He assumed
        that the more you know about subject matter the better you
        would be as a teacher.

SC: But don't say that critically. In those days that was the conven-
        tional wisdom. Would you deny that there was substance to the
        conclusion that school teachers, generally speaking, had a poor
        grasp of the subject matter they taught? That was certainly true in
        the teaching of geography, and there was good reason to believe
        that it was true for other subject matter. Teachers were poorly pre-
        pared. It took the TTT program to get us to face up to the fact
        that knowledge of subject matter was a necessary but not sufficient
        precondition for improving teaching.

SBS: You are right. It took my experience at the Yale Psycho-
        Educational Clinic—when I spent days in classrooms—to see the
        obvious. And when I took the obvious seriously I realized how
        ahistorical I and practically everybody else was, because there had
        been a few individuals, among whom John Dewey towers, who
        told us that as important as knowledge of subject matter was
        knowledge of the ingredients that make for contexts of productive
        learning in general and in the classroom in particular. It was that
        knowledge that was missing.

SC: It was missing. Not missing so much as it was deemphasized or
        simply taken for granted. You used the phrase *contexts of produc-
        tive learning*. What you have to keep in mind is the context of the
        sixties. There was a "fix it" mentality. We were behind the Russians
        in exploring space, racial discrimination was a social virus seem-
        ingly infecting everything, youth were rebelling, cities were
        imploding and exploding, the counterculture made its appearance,
        and test scores were decreasing. Washington was pressured to act.
        People did not complain about an active, big government. They
        wanted action from Washington. Up until the sixties the Office of
        Education was a puny, derogated little agency that always existed
        on a starvation diet. In fact, there was such little regard for the
        Office because it deemphasized subject matter knowledge, that the
        NSF was charged with the responsibility for developing school cur-
        riculum in the Sciences and the Social Science. But when it was
        realized that content could not be separated from teaching if pro-
        ductive learning was to take place, the Office of Education was
        suddenly called in—and hundreds of millions of dollars were
        thrown at it. Almost overnight its growth mushroomed, and it was
        not prepared for it administratively and conceptually. There was no

time to think. Action was the substitute for thinking. And action meant programs that gave promise of fixing things quickly. Government programs suffered from too much money.

SBS: What do you mean by that?

SC: No government agency will at the end of the fiscal year be caught dead saying, "We cannot spend this year's budget wisely, but we would like to carry over an unexpended funds for the purpose, say, of long range planning." That's the way the government works, spend it by July 1 or you lose it. That's not conducive to thinking or, for that matter, honesty. Don Bigelow had no peer when it came to squirreling money in ways the policy makers never intended. In my experience that is also the way it is in state government or in school systems. The idea that you can reform our school systems by the calendar is ridiculous. That is my point: Just as the teaching of a curriculum is driven by the calendar, so is spending. Thinking, at least creative thinking, goes by the boards. It's like when President Bush proclaimed that by the year 2,000 school children will achieve at this or that level of achievement. Famous last words.

SBS: Are you saying that President Bush—or for that matter Nixon, Ford, and Carter—did not understand the complexity of educational reform? With all their advisors?

SC: They did not and could not.

SBS: Could not?

SC: Let me explain because most people don't understand several things about how our political system works in regard to the origins of policy, in this case education, although it is generally the case. Proposals for policy have four major sources: the legislative and the executive branches, governmental agencies, state education lay policy boards, and pressures from special interest groups. Each is a vested interest, and I do not say that pejoratively. Each of them is under pressure to act, each has its own agenda, each sees only part of the problem, each has to appear as if what they propose is *the* answer. If and when a policy is adopted, it is a compromise of sorts with which few are satisfied. But it serves the purpose of appearances: Action is being taken. Now, when this takes place at a time of perceived crisis, thinking, reflecting, and planning are short-circuited, if only again because of time pressures. The fix-it mentality completely overwhelms thinking about preventive efforts. But that is not the point I am trying to make. Each of these sources has layers of influence and responsibility, and as you go up the layers, individuals have less and less knowledge of and experience with the problem a policy seeks to address. Please italicize that. *Ultimate decision-making power far more often than not is with people who have had no first hand experience with the problem.* So between compromise and ignorance, it is a miracle if the adopted policy is realistically adapted to the problem.

SBS: You are saying something I think is very important. Could you illustrate the point in the case of educational reform?

SC: Diane Ravitch had an article in the Autumn 1995 issue of the *American Scholar* entitled "Adventures in Wonderland." She describes her 2 years in the Department of Education. It is both comical and depressing. It is as if the last thing that happens in that department is a discussion of learning and schooling. It is all about power and turfdom. I would bet that most, if not all, of the actors in that department have not been meaningfully involved in a school in years. What she describes is what I observed in the sixties in what was then the Office of Education, and later when it became a department. And that was only one department. The same takes place throughout the government. It is too bad that not many people have read Vice President Gore's publications on Reinventing Government. He describes in amazing, refreshing detail what he calls "the culture of futility." He points out that government is supposed to be sensitive to, to serve, the public, but in the culture of government the problems of the public are abstractions, oversimplified distractions, seen from afar through bureaucratic prisms that prevent seeing the concrete realities of problems.

SBS: You suggested before that the situation is not all that different in public schools. You really think that is so?

SC: It is not that I think so, but I know so from firsthand experience. As a Regent of the New York State Department of Education who chairs both the Elementary, Middle, Secondary, and Continuing Education Committee, and the Commission on Telecommunications and Education, I see what Ravitch and Gore describe. Also, about 15 years ago Mayor Koch asked me to head up a new commission to recommend preschool policy for New York City. What I observed and experienced was as complex, confusing, and frustrating as Northern Ireland, the Mid-East, and Bosnia. And it wasn't peculiar to New York City. When we made our report on what should be taught and where it should be taught, our recommendations on how best to implement the program (which was accepted), we were undermined by the political decision to divide the youngsters equally in programs run by the public schools and Day Care (Human Resources Agency). Forget about holding program implentations to the test of local capacities and experience—the politicians had to satisfy two powerful sets of bureaucratic and political interests in dispensing large sums of money without reference to the well-being of the child or interests of the parent. During the TTT program in the sixties, it was no different in other cities. And about 10 years ago Governor Cuomo asked me to head a special Business-School Alliance. I visited most of the cities in New York, and on a lesser scale and a more quiet one, the people who were the decision makers had no firsthand feel or understanding of the goals of the program. Superintendents would sign on, say it had his or her support, and then give it over to a flunky and wanted to hear no more about it. Every now and then the flunky was a gem. Sheer luck. Sometimes it was someone who did not have enough to do, or whom the superintendent did not respect but could not fire, or, more usually, someone whose title and job were appropriate when in fact that individual was not. In my experience with schools I have to conclude that those who decide on policy far more often than not have no direct knowledge of the problems the policy is supposed to address.

SBS: But isn't it unrealistic to expect that those at or near the top of the hierarchy would have direct knowledge of the different problems that are brought to them? For example, can you expect a superintendent of schools to have knowledge of or direct experience with all educational problems, issues, approaches? Isn't that why he or she has specialized assistants?

SC: Before answering that I have to say something about the obligations of listening and deciding. When you have to decide on a policy, you should feel obliged to be willing and able to listen to those who will be affected by that policy, and that means listening to others besides your assistants. You may not have direct knowledge of the problem but you should be wise enough to know that however bright and objective your assistants may try to be, you cannot, must not, assume that they have sampled well those who will be affected by the new policy. Needless to say, I am not talking about a ritualistic type of listening. If there is anything people down the line want, it is a hearing. If there is anything people in schools complain about is that no one listens to them. I have heard such complaints from students, teachers, principals, and parents. That is why I used the word *oblige*. But it is not only that you owe respect to others, but it is also a protection against deciding on a policy that you will regret.

SBS: Even so, to act in a way you are suggesting requires time, and again, do people on top have that much time?

SC: Now you are getting to where the problem is, and it is particularly a problem in our cities. The larger the organization, the less time there is to listen. The more the administrative layers between top and bottom, the wider the difference between what goes on in the heads of decision makers and those who are at the bottom, the less time there is to listen. There is no getting around that. You hear a lot about bloated bureaucracy in our schools. There are several reasons for that and one of them—and it is only one—is that each layer is supposed to listen to the layers below them. I have read scads of applications from teachers and parents to set up a charter school. And the one thing they have in common is that they want a school where people can meet each other, listen, and decide.

SBS: I cannot agree with you more about size. I consider it a glimpse of the obvious. So why is it that in none of the reports I have read since *A Nation At Risk* is size as a problem hardly discussed?

SC:.   For at least two reasons. The first is that those who sign off on these reports know pitifully little about what you call the culture of schools or school systems. The second reason is that if you take size seriously, it is going to take a lot of money. Why do we have high schools that have two, three, or four thousand students? (Here I partly blame James Bryant Conant and his highly influential Report on the Schools, which argued that comprehensive schools needed to be big enough to be able to offer every conceivable course, rather than the basics. Conant knew a good deal about universities—I don't know how much he knew about schools.) Can you come up with alternatives that will not require more money than we are now spending? Our city high schools are disasters. They are not cost-effective. I consider them breeding grounds for social unrest.

SBS: I am interested in what you said about those who sign off on commission reports whether from the federal government, the states, or foundations. What about boards of education?

SC: That's another can of worms. I admire and respect those who serve on these boards. For the most part their intentions are serious and honorable. But they are, again for the most part, mammothly unsophisticated about the history and substance of the most important issues. I don't expect them to be experts, but should we not expect them to be informed amateurs? For example, discussions about what has been learned about learning and teaching rarely, if ever, take place at board meetings. Size of classes, the length of the school day, the union contract, criteria for expulsion or suspension, standards for promotion or graduation, safety and sex education, budgeting and the like are what they discuss.

SBS: I have pointed that out to friends of mine who have served on boards. Their reply is that in regard to learning and teaching they have to depend on the professionals they hire. One such friend said, "Our most important responsibility is selecting a superintendent who is expert in these matters. We depend on his or her expertise."

SC: Translate what your friend said: "Despite the fact that I am ignorant about the two things that are of bedrock importance, I am able to decide whether the person we hire knows the game and score in these two matters." The first part of the sentence expresses humility. The second expresses, at best, blind hope and prayer, and, at worst, arrogance. I don't say that harshly. That's the position your friend was in. I find it hard to justify decisions based on admitted ignorance.

SBS: Can we shift to the years you were president of Queens College? More specifically, what did you learn about schools and colleges of education?

SC: That is not a simple question. Before I came to Queens I had spent years in the university and had already concluded that the relationship between the university and the public schools was a lopsided one. Simply put, it was that schools existed as places where faculty could do their research and then leave. They felt no responsibility to help schools. That was no less true in colleges of education than it was in, say, psychology or sociology or biology. After all, the reward system in the university has to do with research productivity, not helping organizations like schools. I do not disagree with that. What I disagree with is the snobbishness bordering on contempt for those in educational arena, which is why colleges of education are at or near the bottom on the academic totem pole. It was during the sixties that I came to see how unprepared the social sciences were to comprehend how and why the social change was occurring. They had little to offer in terms of theory, research, or practice. That, it was obvious, was most true in regard to schools and youth. So here was an arena of crucial importance to the public welfare and one to which the social sciences had little to contribute. To me that spoke volumes about how the social sciences understood our society. In that respect I felt the social sciences needed schools as much as schools needed the social sciences.

SBS: What about the physical sciences? Didn't they start getting into the act in the fifties? Were they more responsive than those in the social sciences if only because they were more concerned with maintaining America's superiority in science and technology?

SC: You are making my point. They were the first to see that our schools were our Achilles heel in maintaining our superiority. But they were also the first to expose their naiveté about what schools were like and how they change or don't change. They were well intentioned, but they screwed up with the new math, the new biology, and on and on. They didn't understand learning, teachers, schools, and the change process. You have written a lot about that. But even today I would bet that more hard scientists than social scientists are trying to improve schools.

SBS: So you came to Queens with an agenda?

SC: Not really unless you accept the goal of trying to restore it as a college of unquestionable excellence as a goal. For one thing I came there after the entire college had been decimated, not too strong a word, by the city's fiscal crisis of the seventies. My first job was to restore morale, to assure the faculty that I would do my best to support them in their endeavors, that I was receptive to any idea they had that would improve the atmosphere. But I did have an agenda in regard to the college of education. What I wanted to do was to provide incentives for some faculty members willingly to dirty their hands in the process of school change. I assumed, and it turned out I was right, that there were members of the college of education who wanted to do just that, not only for the purpose of being helpful but to deepen their and our understanding of school change. I arranged with the Chancellor of the school system to provide a modest sum of money that would permit these faculty members—as a group, not as individuals—to seek to be helpful. I convinced him that this could have positive consequences both for the school and college.

SBS: You hoped that it would reinvigorate these members?

SC: I was more hopeful than that. I assumed that if things went well it would positively change our preparatory programs, which certainly needed changing, and would draw other faculty members into the

I.S. 227 project. Between me and the dean of the college of education we chose a couple of people who would have the interest,
creativity, and street smarts to plan and implement the project. By
conventional *academic* standards it has been a huge success. I didn't
tell them what to do or how to do it. I told them they had my
personal interest and support and that I would make available to
them any of our existing resources, which were considerable and
on which you could not put a price. What that project confirmed
in my thinking was the conclusion that unless universities get
involved in our schools neither they nor the schools would change
in appropriate ways. When someone reads the two books that have
come out of that project that person will know what I mean. This
then inspired me to recreate a great high school of excellence—
Townsend Harris—on the Queens College campus. It was small
(1,200 students), the senior year in part was based on college-level
courses taught by high school and college faculty jointly, and it
combined the classical (Latin is required) and the modern (all students are science and computer literate) traditions. It's a reincarna-
tion of the Townsend Harris that Mayor LaGuardia closed in 1942
for being too elite, and reflects my experiences of the 1930s and
early 1940s as a student at one of the country's other elite
schools—the Boston Public Latin School.

SBS: Why did you decide to leave Queens?

SC: Because despite the many virtues of the city's college-university
system, it is a bureaucratic, frustrating system, and I no longer
wanted to be in a role where I was increasingly frustrated by
forces, vested interests, and power struggles. In line with what I
said earlier, the size of the college-university system guarantees
frustration, alienation, and burnout. I quit while I was ahead.

SBS: You have been a Regent of the State of New York, the overseer of
the state's educational system. What new things have you learned?

SC: My answer will surprise you: I have learned little that is new. But it
certainly has given me a breadth and depth of experience that confirms the major points I made earlier.

SBS: For example.

SC: Well, for starters, anyone who thinks that state and local systems
are apolitical oases concerned only with learning and teaching can
probably be convinced to buy the Brooklyn Bridge. Both are
enmeshed in the political system with negative consequences out-
weighing the positive ones. Second, there were nearly 7,000
employees in the state department of education, some of whom

are in Albany and a similar number in the New York City Board of Education more than four hundred miles away (the figure is rapidly declining owing to recent budget cuts). The distance, interpersonally and geographically, between the Chancellor and New York City Board of Education and the Regents with its Commissioner and Department of Education, on the one hand, and the layers of administration in the department on the other, is vast and for all practical purposes unbridgeable. I am not calling anybody a villain. I am saying that size and distance inevitably create major problems. Finally, whatever I said earlier about boards of education is true—it has to be true—for the Regents.

SBS: There is a conclusion I have come to listening to what you have said: The way our schools are governed both by the state and local communities is in need of drastic overhaul. Do you agree?

SC: I agree. But do you have a better alternative?

SBS: That's what I am thinking about.

SC: We need dreamers. But I know you know that if and when your ideas ever get a hearing, you and I will not be around.

SBS: When I want the truth I'll ask you for it. That I have always counted on.

VIEW C

For the past several years I have kept a file of published interviews with and speeches of governors known for their interest in and policies for educational reform. Also, I have tried to see TV programs, usually on PBS or C-Span, on which elected officials discuss school improvement. The following interview is fictional. I have tried here to focus on those issues common to what these different individuals most often express.

SBS: I want to thank you for granting me this hour with you. I know what a busy schedule you have. But I asked for this hour because you are regarded as one of the few governors who puts school improvement very high on your agenda.

Gov: Frankly, ordinarily I would have asked the state's chief educational officer to answer your letter and invite you to talk with her. But you were very clear that you wanted to talk only with me because of the leadership I have exercised in educational reform. You may be surprised to learn that you are the first academic who has written to me not because you were "selling" something and wanted me to get on board but rather because you wanted to know how I came to have the views I hold. To be completely honest, I checked you out and was told you were not flaky. So don't be surprised if I try to interview you.

SBS: That's okay with me. I have never been interviewed by any public official, let alone a governor. I did write a book titled *Letters to a Serious Educational President,* my fictional president having been elected in the year 2000 and who put schooling at the very top of his agenda. Copies were sent to President Clinton and the Secretary of Education. In a serendipitous way I found out from a friend who had a one-on-one meeting with the secretary that my book was well marked up. I allowed myself to hope that he would ask to meet with me but I never did hear from him.

Gov: In that book were you telling him what he should do? That would be the kiss of death.

SBS: I was "selling" him two ideas, one of which was that he already knew what I was selling, that he would agree with me, but that he wasn't taking what he already knew seriously. I was not telling him anything he didn't know from personal experience. And what he knew you know.

Gov: And I am not taking it seriously either?

SBS: Yes.

Gov: So what were you selling him?

SBS: Can we postpone my answer for a while at least? Consistent with what I say in that book, my answer will make more sense to you if I know where you are coming from.

Gov: Fair enough. It's a sound political strategy to know where people are coming from and why before you attempt to influence them.

SBS: You catch on quickly. Can we start by briefly telling me what your agenda for school reform was and is and why?

Gov: I am glad you said was and is. The first thing I did was search for a new chief education officer who could exercise leadership, shake up the department, and advise me how I can accomplish what I think needs to be done. When I go to the legislature I want to be sure I have evidence that what needs to be done can and should be done.

SBS: You were not satisfied with the previous chief officer?

Gov: During the election campaign I left nobody in doubt about how I felt about the state department and my predecessor, both of whom tinkered with the fringes of the problems. I was advocating long overdue, bold actions. So when I was elected, the chief officer resigned, giving me the opportunity to appoint the kind of person I needed.

SBS: I don't envy her for what she was up against.

Gov: What do you mean?

SBS: What if you were a member of a department the incoming governor had criticized for being lackluster and unimaginative? How would you regard the white knight in armor appointed to shake up the department?

Gov: How else could I get them to change, to move in new directions? I had faith that the person I appointed could remotivate them. Don't tell me that I should not have done what I did.

SBS: Far from it. You did what you should have done and I applaud it. My point is that you and your appointee had to expect that x number of people in that department would not be enthusiastic and many would be hostile. For all I know your appointee may have handled the situation well.

Gov: I think she did, although I have to admit that she was frustrated by not being able to get rid of some people or change their responsibilities or to get them to be more helpful to her. But that is par for the course. For example, some employees went to their favorite legislator and complained that my appointee was authoritarian, was not abiding by personnel policies of the state, was alienating local school districts, and on and on. Needless to say, those legislators complained to me. The first policy for which I was going to seek legislative approval concerned a new and more equitable basis for state aid to city and suburban school districts. For reasons I hope are obvious to you, I had said little about that in my campaign. I knew what a can of worms that was. When I was elected, the first thing I told my appointee was to come up with a more equitable plan. Well, before that plan was really developed there was an uproar from the suburbs. My appointee had good reason to believe that members of the department were leaking the plan to people they knew in the suburbs. She was not being paranoid.

SBS: What you are saying is grist for the mill of those critics who indict a bloated education bureaucracy.

Gov: I know. But what the critics don't know, or if they know they do not say out loud, is that it is no less true in all parts of state government. It's built into our system of governance. I have to say, however, that the state department of education may be the least helpful, at least in my experience, although it is not all their fault.

SBS: What do you mean by that?

Gov: For example, if you were to put together all the bills enacted by the legislature in the past 10 years that affect every school district, you would have a big book. Some of these laws concern finances; others, broadly speaking, concern what has to be taught; others are about licensing, termination, tenure, and appeal procedures; then there are those laws concerning safety, building codes, and transportation; then, of course, there are laws that spell out the supervisory, advisory, data gathering responsibilities of the department. And when you add to those laws—each requiring the department to develop rules and regulations—what is required to receive, administer, and dispense federal funds for this or that program, you have a large, balkanized department. Just to administer state and federal programs for handicapped children is one big affair, if only because they inevitably contain issues about parental rights, educational–medical–psychological procedures and judgment, and departmental oversight.

SBS: It sounds like one big accounting, filing, paper pushing, policing operation.

Gov: In large measure it is. And that is why local school districts don't see the department as a source of help but rather as one big pain in the neck, a kind of insensitive, problem-producing Big Brother. Remember, we are a big state. There is no way the department can know what is going on in most districts. They don't have the time; it is not set up for them to have time. They live in their encapsulated world figuring out ways to keep me and the legislature off their backs. I know more about what is going on in school districts than the department does, and I don't know as much as I should. At least it is set up so that I should know. I am the governor, a politician, and that means I am always on the campaign trail, even after I have just been elected.

SBS: If my newspaper file on you is correct, your next important initiative was for parent advisory councils at each school.

Gov: Correct, except that what I really wanted was for each school to have the equivalent of a board of directors comprised of the principal, three teachers, and four parents. They would be the policy makers for each school: the selection of teachers and principals and the ultimate authority for everything else that impacts on a school.

SBS: What was your rationale for that?

Gov: In one word: accountability. For one thing, school personnel do
        not have a good track record for management, innovation, and
        educational outcomes. That is especially true in our cities where
        morale is low and conflict between minority groups and school
        personnel is omnipresent. I wanted to put an end to a situation
        where the community blames the school and the school blames
        the parents and the larger community. If the community wants
        better schools, then it should actively participate in decision mak-
        ing. How else can parents in a community become informed about
        why things are not going well and what the options are for
        improving their school? Let's say that in school x the governing
        board is in agreement about what should be done but there are
        obstacles stemming from the school system's rules and regulations
        and priorities. Or the obstacles came from what the state does or
        does not do or prescribe. Well, it makes a difference if the govern-
        ing board of the school yells, shouts, protests, and pressures or if
        the parents alone or the school personnel alone try to change
        things. What the educators have trouble comprehending is that on
        their own they are far less influential than if they are allied with the
        parents, and vice versa.

SBS: In other words, you saw it as a virtue that your plan would lead to
        a different type of conflict: the governing board versus the
        hierarchy on the board of education, or the board and the state
        department.

Gov: You just said out loud what I could not say publicly.

SBS: Aren't you implicitly criticizing, among other things, boards of
        education? After all, if schools are far from what we want them to
        be, should we not direct some blame to boards of education?

Gov: Of course. I was on my town's board of education for 6 years.
        That was much earlier in my life. I learned a helluva lot. First,
        school systems are part of the political system. Second, school
        boards are completely dependent on the superintendent and his or
        her assistants for what is going on in the system. Third, whatever
        knowledge we were given was partial knowledge. Fourth, if you
        were the kind of person who made it easy for people to approach
        you, and if they felt you were trustworthy, you realized how much
        you didn't know about what was going on—some good things
        and some bad things—and if you were not seen as accessible, you
        found out a lot at the board's open meetings where parents gave
        the board a piece of their mind.

SBS: In light of what you have said about state departments of education and boards, it is hard for me to avoid the conclusion that whatever their virtues they are at least matched by some inherent inadequacies. We cannot count on them for leadership, innovation, and effective management. Am I reading you wrongly?

Gov: I have never thought about it in that way. I suppose I accept the governance system as it is and try to improve it. I have never thought about an alternative system. Have you?

SBS: I'm trying to. At this point my thinking is not all that clear because, like you, I have spent all of my adult life unreflectively assuming that the governance system of our schools was philosophically and politically the best system. So, again like you, I have trouble coming up with alternatives.

Gov: You have given me something to think about. The fact is that I will not have time to think—really to think—until I leave office.

SBS: I diverted you from finishing your account about parent participation and equality in decision making in schools. You said that the legislation that was enacted called for parents to be only in advisory roles. How come the change?

Gov: That's easy to answer. As you know, school teachers and school administrators have very strong and effective lobbies. And members of boards of education, precisely because of their connection with the political system, have ways of putting pressure on the legislature. So when my proposal became public these groups went into action. They used three arguments. First, they were not opposed to parents in an advisory role. Second, they were already moving to give parents more of a role. Third, what I was proposing reflected the contempt I had for the knowledge, experience, and judgment of educators. I expected resistance and criticism. I had explained to the leaders of the two parties why I thought my proposal was in the best interest of educators and parents, and many of them agreed with me. But when the shit hit the fan, I simply didn't have the votes. I had to compromise. So we have advisory boards. I took what I could get. Politics is the art of the possible. Another way to put it is that it is about power and reality.

SBS: That defeat must have angered you.

Gov: Not really. Remember, I expected opposition. I underestimated its strength. Surprisingly, however, at that same session of the legislature they went along with me on setting up some charter schools and allowing people who had specialized work experience but no formal training as teachers to begin teaching before they enrolled in preparatory programs.

SBS: How come you had the votes for those programs? I would have thought that those who opposed you earlier would have also been opposed to those programs that were a break with tradition.

Gov: They were opposed but what the teachers, administrators, and boards of education underestimated was the depth of the frustration and anger people generally feel about what they see as an educational bureaucracy—in the state department and in our cities—which stifles new ideas, is self-serving, and always feathering its own nest. It's similar to the way the general public has come to regard the medical and legal communities: They are part of the problem, not of the solution. The idea that a public school would for all practical purposes be free of state department's book of rules, regulations, and procedures was appealing. Besides, at the beginning the number of such schools would be small.

SBS: I know my time with you is limited, and there is one question I want to put to you, a question that to my knowledge you have never addressed.

Gov: I feel a criticism coming on.

SBS: I intend no criticism at all. Indeed, if I were a member of the legislature, I would have enthusiastically supported you in all you wanted to accomplish. My question is a simple one. You may even think that the answer is so self-evident that I must be extraordinarily dense to ask it.

Gov: You are beginning to sound like an Ivy League academic.

SBS: There are more than a few people who see me that way.

Gov: So what is the question?

SBS: Why do you think that your initiatives will affect educational outcomes in a positive way?

Gov: I'm confused. You said you would have supported my initiatives. Why would you have supported me if you didn't think they would have positive educational effects?

SBS: In the case of changing the state's formula for aid to cities and suburbs, I would have supported you on principles of equity and humaneness. There are city schools in scandalous physical conditions. In some cities they are lacking in books for each student or using books that are glaringly out of date, if they were ever in date. I would have supported you on parent participation in decision making on the basis of the political principle: If you are going to be affected by a decision, you should stand in some relationship to that decision. If teachers and parents agree that they will take the responsibility for a school that they think will be better for children than the schools they now attend, I would be supportive because I favor experimenting, i.e., giving new ideas a hearing, assuming, of course, they are not off the wall. But in none of these instances would my support reflect the belief they recognized and were addressing the most basic problem.

Gov: Which is, professor?

SBS: What are the features of contexts for productive learning, and do they exist in our modal classrooms? In a number of books I argue—monotonously some would say—that those features do not exist, indeed cannot exist, in classrooms as they are now organized in schools as they are organized.

Gov: That is as sweeping a statement as I have ever heard. It is also one of the most depressing and—I have to say it the way I think it— very arrogant because you are saying that you know a basic issue that no one else in your profession does.

SBS: In light of the way I said it, I can understand why you said what you just said. The fact is that what I said is the basic issue has been said clearly by others as far back as 200 years ago. I claim no originality whatsoever. Briefly, and without the usual and necessary qualifications, productive learning requires that you know and start with the interests, curiosities, and questions in the mind of the young learner, which are always concrete, personal, and motivating. You do not start with a predetermined, calendar-driven curriculum. The artistry of the teacher inheres in his or her ability to use that starting point to widen the learner's horizons, to help the child willingly to become motivated to learn what you want that child to learn. It is an artistry that is always sensitive and responsive to where the child is and, no less important, to any gulf between where the child is and where you are. It is an artistry that requires not only an understanding of young minds but also when or where the logical steps or concepts of the subject matter can be problems for the learner. Those steps or concepts are abstractions; the minds of young learners are very concrete.

Gov: That strikes me as common sense. A lot of parents, certainly not all, know that. My wife and I learned that with our first child whom we were always seeing in terms of the child-rearing books we read and reread, except that he didn't quite fit the picture. He didn't always react the way he was "supposed" to. He had his own style, and we made mistakes because we were young, going by the book, and resisting his style. Finally, we said the hell with it, we will do it his way.

SBS: You've got the point.

Gov: And you are saying that common sense is not used in the classroom? I find that hard to believe.

SBS: I would have been surprised if you thought otherwise. Can you spare me a couple more minutes so that I can leave you with two things to think about, for each of which there is hard evidence?

Gov: Go ahead.

SBS: First, in the modal 45- to 50-minute classroom in, say, social studies the average number of questions asked by students is two, and sometimes it is one kid asking the two questions. Second, as you go up the grades—elementary to middle to high schools—students show less and less interest in school learning. There is more than one reason for each of these findings. We are dealing with a complicated problem for which there is no simple explanation. Nevertheless, the conclusion is justified that classrooms are not places where the context for productive learning exists.

Gov: You have given me something to think about.

SBS: I hope so. Thanks for giving me your time.

Gov: Wait a minute. I was intrigued by your phrase "the calendar-driven curriculum."

SBS: You can teach by the calendar. You cannot learn by it.

Gov: Intuitively the implications of that are mind boggling.

SBS: It is. Once you pursue those implications, you may regret it.

Gov: Why do you say that?

SBS: Because you will see how counterproductive the present situation is and why the reform movement was doomed, however well-intentioned it was and is.

The Non-Learning,
Non–Self-Correcting System

I n recent years I have been asking people this question: Are you satisfied
with the present governance system of public education? The answers were
a qualified yes. The qualifications had to do with financing, inadequate
educational outcomes, community–parent participation, regionalism, and
the bureaucratic mentality. No one questioned the system *qua* system, i.e.,
the need for, the powers of, and interrelationships among a state department of education, a local board of education, a superintendent of schools,
a principal, teachers, colleges and universities, and parents. As one person
put it, "Politically and philosophically it is in principle a democratic system
that can accommodate to a variety of needed changes. If it doesn't work as
well as we like, it says less about the system and more about the people in it
and the strong conflicting social pressures impacting on it." There were a
few individuals who were so deeply critical of the system and its outcomes
that they were disposed "to give up on it," although all but one of them could
offer no alternative. The one exception was a person who semifacetiously said,
"Let's privatize the whole shebang." It will come as no surprise to the reader
that no one with whom I talked expressed any optimism whatsoever that, generally speaking, schools would discernibly improve. That was true whether

or not the respondent was an educator, another type of professional, or an ordinary citizen. It was difficult for most of them to explain or justify their pessimism. It was the feeling that "something was wrong somewhere," but they could be no more specific than that. Some indicated that much was amiss in our society, and schools were no exception.

These answers were predictable. Leaving the educational arena aside, the literature on organizational change is replete with instances where the approach has been to change personnel or to change the perspective of existing personnel, or to improve speed and quality of communication between and among levels of authority, or to provide incentives for increased motivation and commitment, or to adopt a more equitable reward system, or to alter who should participate in what ways and to what degree in decision making, or all of these. Frequently these may require changes in the organizational chart by changing or eliminating boxes in that chart or by changing the directions of arrows indicating how the boxes should be in relation to each other. Although these changes are intended as "systemic" ones, far more often than not they hardly alter the hierarchy of power despite the rhetoric of power flowing down-up as well as top-down. That, I hasten to add, does not mean that no changes take place but rather that little or no changes take place in the basic features of the system. There is a difference between a new system and changes within an existing system. I should also add that I am in no way implying that a new system is inherently virtuous. When the Bolsheviks gained power in the Russian revolution, they changed the system of governance and for 70 years ruled the country in a tyrannical, murderous fashion. They sought escape from a Czarist tyranny and in short order instituted their own brand. Whether in the political, business, or educational arenas, to be in favor of system change does not automatically confer brownie points on you; the verdicts of history are about consequences, not motivations. Henry Ford introduced the assembly line system in industrial production, and he paid his workers what was then a high daily wage, five dollars a day. He was considered an organizational genius pointing the way to a rosy, prosperous, technological future. Today we think otherwise because we see the assembly line as a cruel, insensitive, debilitating enslavement of workers to an ever-moving production line. Henry Ford's ideas impacted on and were emulated by educators and others in the then political–social–educational establishment. More about that later. Suffice it to say here, his overarching criterion justifying his system of production—and he did have such a criterion—was increasing production at ever lowering costs. His overarching criterion said little or nothing about the lives of workers.

Let us turn to an instructive, more heartening example quite relevant to this book. I refer (as I always do) to the constitutional convention of 1787. That convention initially was intended to repair the dangerous inadequacies of the Articles of Confederation. (Indeed, when Thomas Jefferson learned that his friend James Madison was supporting the move to scrap the Articles of Confederation and come up with a new system of governance, he was surprised and somewhat opposed to such a departure.) What the convention came up with was a new system of governance, unlike anything in history. What is most relevant to my present purposes is that the new system of governance had one overarching goal: how to harmonize political power with individual freedom. Put in another way: Given all that history contains about power, its uses and misuses, its necessity and yet the necessity to constrain it, what system of governance stands a chance of securing individual liberties by allocating, distributing, and constraining the exercise of power? That was the central problem and one that was morally, politically, and realistically complex, which explains why that convention occupied several months, during which scores of proposals were discarded, examined and reexamined, compromises arrived at, compromises undone. If they did not need to be taught about how political power could be abused, they also did not have to be taught that the citizenry, as individuals and in groups, did not always make wise and reasoned decisions. They were not devotees of the concept of rational man (women were not in the picture). They were not armchair theorists. They were practical men confronting a historically vexing problem. And when they were through, they were far from certain that the new system of governance would achieve its central purpose. They included an amending process in the final document. And in order to secure approval, it was later necessary to include a Bill of Rights that made individual rights more explicit.

This book is an attempt to start from scratch, to come up with a system of governance of education which has one overarching goal (which I will come to shortly). Ideally, such an attempt should be made by a group of knowledgeable people willing and able to give the time to such an effort. I have made that suggestion before (Sarason, 1993b; 1995b), not because the product of such an effort would have impact but rather because it *might* give currency to issues that need to be confronted. That my suggestion had all of the ballast of a lead balloon in no way surprised me. But I tried in the only way available to me, i.e., writing, hectoring. I did not resist writing this book because I was devoid of ideas and suggestions. My resistance derived from the knowledge that the problem was too multifaceted to be dealt with by one individual. What is so instructive about the constitutional convention of 1787, and explains its length, is the interplay, the clash, the creativity of ideas and personalities. What kept them together was the acknowledged brute fact that the Articles of Confederation were dangerously inadequate. When they were through, no one was completely satisfied but all could live with the compromise. We are still in their debt.

What follows in this book is informed by several considerations, assumptions, judgments.

1. Education has multiple goals, but not all goals are equally important. How should we scale these goals, and having scaled them how should governance of education take seriously and support the ordering of the priorities?

2. There is one goal that, if not achieved, makes the achievement of all other goals very unlikely. That goal is to create those conditions that make students *want* to learn; *not* have to learn but *want* to learn more about self, others, and the world. The overarching purpose of schooling and its governance is to support that goal, i.e., to create and sustain contexts of productive learning supportive of the natural curiosity and wonder with which children start schooling.

3. Contexts for productive learning are no arcane mystery. They require that adults start with where the child is: his or her curiosities, questions, puzzlements. The artistry of teaching inheres in how to capitalize on that starting point so as to enlarge and support what the child *wants* to learn. That is to say, you seek to help the child forge connections between what he or she wants to know and what the child needs to learn. I say artistry because those connections cannot be forged by a fiat that requires the child to conform to a predetermined or calendar driven program. You can teach by the calendar, you cannot learn productively by the calendar. This is not permissiveness or a mindless indulgence of a child's whims and fancies. It is a way of "hooking" the child, enlarging the child's view in line with the maxim that the more you know the more you need to know.

4. Teachers cannot create and sustain contexts for productive learning unless those contexts exist for them. Teaching is not a once-and-for-all learned craft. It is (should be) a developmental process that today is hindered by teachers being in an encapsulated classroom with no time, opportunity, or forums where the issues and problems of teaching are discussed, not in the abstract but in terms of concrete children and teachers. To be helped and stimulated by others, or to stimulate and help others, requires forums where that is expected and possible. If teaching is a developmental process, it must also be a self-correcting one. Contexts for productive learning are as necessary for teachers as they are for students. Where they exist for neither—which is generally the case today—you get learning but not productive learning: the sense that one's understanding is being enlarged and propelling one willingly to the future.

5. Bedrock to a system of governance should be the political principle: If any one or any group is going to be affected by a policy, they should have some role in the formulation and decisions about that policy.

This book will not sit well with those who believe that the existing governance system of education is rescuable. It is not rescuable if by that is meant that it can be restored to an earlier state of grace and efficacy. It never was an efficacious system. It arose largely as a way to tame and socialize the children of scores of millions of immigrant children. The concept of individuality and productive learning was never in the picture. What was in the picture was rote learning, memorization, drill according to a predetermined calendar-driven curriculum to which the student had to conform. It was basically a shape up or ship out approach in which being shipped out could mean not being allowed in school, or being segregated in special classes, programs, or tracks from which one could never emerge. They were "rejects" from an assembly line of education, rejects in no way interpreted as casting any negative light on the system. There were always a few educators who saw the system for what it was: an educational factory in which a student's interests, curiosities, questions were of no account. Schools were contrived oases from real life and that included the life of the mind; the life of the mind and the social life outside of the oases were off limits, i.e., interferences to what a child *had* to learn. In the reigning pedagogy individuality and productive learning were foreign concepts.

As time went by the rhetoric of individuality and productive learning gained currency, less because of the power of ideas and more because the children of immigrants were not content to have their children receive an education that consigned them, as it had their parents, to lives of drudgery. Following World War II, *and precisely because of that war* (Sarason, 1966), the inadequacies and failures of the public schools could not be kept off the societal agenda. The era of educational reform had begun. Whereas earlier movements for educational reform came in cycles—every ten years or so cries for reform were sounded and curricula changed—educational reform now took on an urgency and degree of continuity as never before. As one looks back over the post–World War II era, one cannot avoid the conclusion that it was an era of increasing disappointment with and criticism of the efficacy of the public schools, and that is putting it mildly. Although the rhetoric of individuality and productive learning was increasingly heard and taken seriously in a classroom here and a classroom there, a school here and a school there, it was neither taken seriously, let alone implemented, in schools generally. And in the case of the minuscule number of exceptions, they occurred despite, not because of, the system. My own experience, as well as a review of the literature on educational reform, substantiates the conclusion that these exceptions traversed a minefield of obstacles in order to survive, and many did not survive.[1]

I am in no way suggesting a conspiracy against the concepts of individuality and productive learning. Indeed, I have never met an educator, a public official, or a citizen who argued against the primacy of these concepts. Rather, I am making two points. First, there is a reluctance or inability to pursue the *practical* implications of these concepts. Second, when they are seriously pursued, it becomes obvious that the existing governance structure would require such a radical overhaul as to be regarded as an indulgence of utopian thinking. If by utopian thinking is meant the exercise of imagination to depict situations that do not and cannot now exist, what I have said (and will say throughout this book) is not utopian. There are instances, albeit few, in some public and private schools where the concepts are taken seriously and appropriately implemented. They do not exist in a never-never land; they exist today, e.g., the school created and recently described by Weinstein and Butterworth (1996). And the knowledgeable reader knows that it is these concepts that are powering the movement for charter schools, which is an effort to get these schools "out from under" the present governance system. And, I must reiterate, there is no reformer who leaves us in any doubt that the success of his or her efforts requires a governance change. Unfortunately, none of these reformers confront the governance system as a system that includes the school, the school system or district, the board of education, the state department of education, the university, parents, the legislature, and the executive branch of government. These are stakeholders in a very complicated educational system. They are not passive stakeholders; they have similar but by no means identical interests and agendas; more often than not they are in conflict with and mistrust each other. *It is a system so balkanized as to prevent meaningful discussion of, let alone agreement about, educational goals and priorities. It is not a system that can initiate and sustain meaningful reform.* On the contrary, its features are such as to make reform extraordinarily difficult and even impossible. Under severe and unusual pressure it may permit tinkering, even the appearance of reform, but as time goes on and the pressures decrease, the leadership changes, the tinkering and the reform lose force and purpose, confirming the adage that the more things change the more they remain the same. *It is not a self-correcting system; there are no means, procedures, forums through which the system "learns."* It is a system with a seemingly infinite capacity to remain the same in the face of obvious inadequacies, unmet goals, and public dissatisfaction. *It is a system in which accountability is so diffused that no one is accountable. It is a system that has outlived all of its reformers, and will outlive the present generation of reformers.* I made that prediction 30 years ago, and I have no reason to think otherwise today.

We are not used to thinking in system terms. We hear much about the need for "systemic" reform and what is almost always meant is either some kind of change in a single school or in a single school district. Sometimes, but not always, the called-for change involves altering power relationships or giving greater autonomy in policy making or resource allocation to the individual school, or both. I heartily endorse such goals but only on the basis of the political principle: Those who are going to be affected by an educational policy should have some role in the formulation and implementation of the policy (Sarason, 1995b). But why should such changes be expected favorably to affect educational outcomes? That question hardly receives an answer. What is implied is that by changing power relationships, teachers and others will be more creative, more willing to be bold in thinking and action, and, therefore, the quality and level of student learning will be enhanced. To the extent that existing power relationships destroy, as they do, the morale of teachers by reducing them to the level of alienated ciphers, changing those relationships may have positive effects on teachers. But, again, why will those changes have positive effects on students? And the answer is that unless those changes specifically and concretely focus on individuality and productive learning, there will not be such positive effects on students. To seek to change power relationships ("systemic" reform) without those changes being in the service of clear conceptions of individuality and productive learning is a missed opportunity. Put in another way, changing power relationships is a necessary but *not* sufficient basis for improving the quality and context of learning. For example, in an increasing number of states parents, by legislative fiat, have been given parity with educators in educational decision making. From personal observation as well as reports I received from observers, there has been no change whatsoever in regard to taking seriously individuality and productive learning. Needless to say, teachers viewed such legislation as another instance, either of taking pot shots at teachers or blaming the victim or both. But, again in my experience, the story is only slightly better when teachers have asked for and been given a greater voice in decision making in their school. In most instances, what passes for site-based management is a charade. In a few instances it is not a charade, but they are instances where the teachers learned rather quickly that taking individuality and productive learning seriously was impossible given the nature of the larger system. They lowered their sights.

I do not relish being perceived as a wet blanket or as someone who, if he cannot have the whole loaf would rather eat nothing. Basic to my stance are two brute facts. First, the educational reform movement in the post–World War II era has been, generally speaking, a failure. That is not to deny that we have learned a lot but rather that the system has not "learned" the lessons to be drawn from that history. And the second fact is that the reform movement has not dealt with the stakeholders who are part of the system and who play crucial roles, directly or indirectly, in setting goals and priorities. More correctly, these stakeholders and their relationship to the system insure that the important issues will be obscured. To put it bluntly, the system is incapable of confronting the sources of its inadequacies. Far from being a self-correcting system, it is a problem-producing one.

There was a time when the defects of the system were seen as deriving from a lack of financial resources. Today, few hold that position. Beginning with the 1954 desegregation decision, the moral dimensions of the system's inadequacies could no longer be ignored. It was then that we began to hear that the overarching goal of the system was "to help *each* child realize his or her potential." That, it turned out, was (and is) empty rhetoric because no one saw fit to raise the question: Is the system capable of taking the concepts of individuality and productive learning seriously? There was a period, by no means over, when the chief culprits were seen to be teachers who had an inadequate grasp of the subject matter they taught. As is so often the case, that blame assignment confirmed the adage that it is hard to be completely wrong. It also confirmed Mencken's caveat that for every problem there is a simple answer that is wrong. How does a teacher's increased grasp of subject matter get communicated to and absorbed by students so that it is psychologically "owned" by them and motivates them to *want* to learn more? On what basis can one claim that teachers' increased grasp of subject matter is *alone* adequate to deal with the fact that as students go from elementary to middle to high school their desire for learning steadily decreases? Does what we have learned about child development tell us nothing about contexts of productive learning?

With one exception, every major reform effort accepts the system as it is, which is why I have predicted, and continue to predict, they will have little or no general impact or staying power. The one exception is the charter school, which is by legislative fiat *relatively* independent of the system. They are minuscule in number. They are too new to justify passing judgment on them. From what I have read or have been told their rationale takes seriously the concepts of individuality and productive learning. My concern is threefold. First, will they implement their rationale appropriately and consistently? Second, because they are *relatively* free of the existing condition, will they be able to resist efforts "to bring them into line?" Third, will they be able to discharge their obligation candidly and inform the general public about what they are doing, experiencing, learning, and accomplishing? The third point is the most important one because if inadequately dealt with, we end up with an "experiment" from which we learn nothing, an old story in the history of educational reform. One would (should) expect that in a major departure from traditional practice—a departure of great *potential* value—resources would be provided adequately and impartially to discharge the reporting function. As best as I can judge, those resources are not in the picture. What would be surprising would be if they were in the picture. The legislature and executive branches of state government—who, let us not forget, are stakeholders in the educational system—have never understood, or have been helped to understand, that the reforms they initiate or approve will not serve the public interest unless they and we have a secure basis for passing judgment, i.e., how, when, and why predictable and unpredictable problems arose and how they were dealt with, what self-correcting actions or procedures were employed, etc. I have no doubt that legislators and executives in state and federal government approve of the Federal Drug Administration's practice of not making a drug available for public use until there is a good, impartial basis for concluding that the drug achieves its intended, positive effects. But that understanding and approval by elected officials does not transfer to the educational arena, which is what I meant when I said that the existing governance structure of education is not capable of self-correction or learning. On a purely actuarial basis, I am skeptical that over time charter schools will remain an exception to what I said earlier.

In the chapters that follow I attempt to describe features of a new governance system for education. I do so for several reasons. First, I have long been a critic of the existing system. Second, it took me years to confront the fact that the system was not rescuable. Third, the inadequacies of the system are having percolating, negative consequences throughout our society, especially in our cities where issues of race and poverty force me to regard cities as time bombs. Fourth, despite the fact that people knowledgeable about education, to say the least, have grave doubts about the system, I have been singularly unsuccessful in getting funding sources and/or the powers that be to take actions that would give currency to the need for a different system. Fifth, despite my unsuccessful efforts I feel obliged to, so to speak, go it alone. I do not do so with a firm sense of security that what I have come up will be clear or compelling or as comprehensive as it should be. If it stimulates discussion and debate, or if it leads others to come up with better alternatives, my effort will not have been in vain. Time is not on our side. Public dissatisfaction with the existing system is real and deep. In the quiet of their nights most people know there is something very wrong with the existing system.

I entreat the reader to assume the obligation to try to take distance from the system as it now is. That is a lot to ask of readers who, like me, have been socialized to regard the system as if it had been given to us on an educational Mount Sinai. It was not easy for me, and it will not be easy for the reader. But the time to use whatever conceptual creativity we possess is now.

NOTES

[1]There are two "literatures": the published and the unpublished, the latter consisting of efforts that were aborted for a variety of reasons, among the most frequent being a nonsupportive governance structure. As countless teachers and administrators (mostly principals) have told me, the governance structure and culture rewards conformity, not courage and risk taking. "No good deed goes unpunished"—that sums up almost all that I observed and was told. What I call the unpublished literature is far larger than the published one.

CHAPTER III

The Context of Productive Learning

We say that Jimmy has learned to walk. Ordinarily we do not examine that statement, let alone challenge what our eyes tell us. It does not occur to us that the statement is true, incomplete, and misleading. If challenged, we will not deny that, for the biologically intact youngster, learning to walk is not an inevitable outcome. We can imagine scandalous conditions where that youngster does not and cannot learn to walk. Because the organism is programmed with the potential to learn to walk does not mean he or she will learn to walk. Whether the organism learns to walk, and when, depends on a host of factors external to the child, factors we tend to take for granted. Long before the child walks, he or she sees people walking; the child experiences how different the world looks lying in the crib and after being picked up; most children know the difference between being picked up and held by a stranger and by a familiar parent; the infant who begins to try to crawl hears the approving reactions of others; having learned to crawl, that child may be held by the parent and encouraged and helped to "go through the motions" of walking, an encouragement intended to stimulate the child to want to walk; it is taken for granted that the child wants to walk, i.e., walking is not foisted on the child. In brief, learning to walk has a complicated history of interpersonal transactions in which the "environment" explicitly assumes that: (1) The child can learn to walk; (2) The child wants to or will want to walk; and (3) It is the obligation of adults to help the child go from wanting to walk to being able to walk. "You have to know how to walk before you can run"—that can be translated to mean "first things first": You start where the child is and you bring him or her along to where you want the child to be able to go. So, when we say that a child has learned to walk we mean, or should mean, that others have operated on the assumption that the child wants to learn to walk. It is a cooperative, mutually reinforcing developmental process in which the child is by no means the sole agent.

Take toilet training (which many parents would rather not take!). The parent knows that at some point the child will be capable of being toilet trained. The parent knows three other things: (1) The point is not predictable; (2) There will be no one-trial learning; and (3) The pace of the learning will be determined by the strength of the child's desire to learn. Parents differ wildly in how seriously they take items 2 and 3. If some parents know that toilet training cannot be achieved overnight, there are more than a few parents who adopt an unrealistic time perspective and, when that interacts with a misevaluation of the strength of the child's desire to want to be toilet trained, the parent begins the foisting, demanding process that can be quite stormy and counterproductive. To ask a child to give up urinating and defecating whenever or wherever it pleases him or her is to ask a lot. There are many factors that determine the strength of a child's willingness to start the toilet training process, but among the most important, I would say *the* most important, is loving and wanting to please the parent. Whatever complicates or interferes with that wanting interferes with wanting to learn to be toilet trained, i.e., the parent does not start with where the child is, the parent starts with a predetermined lesson plan.

Why do parents buy toys for their child, picking toys the parents think will interest and stimulate and child and are appropriate to his or her level of motor coordination? Why do some parents hang a mobile above the crib? The brief answer is that the parents seek not only to engage the child's attention and interests but to aid the child to gain a sense of control and competence over his or her actions. As the infant develops, parents are (or should be) alert to signs that the child's interests and actions are expanding, suggesting that toys of increasing difficulty might be introduced. Toy manufacturers do not say that this or that toy is, say, for an 18-month-old child; they will say that it is appropriate for children between 18 and, say, 30 months of age. That range is by way of indicating that it is the parents' obligation to determine when and if their child is "ready" for that toy. At the very least the implicit message is: "Do you have reason to believe that your child will want to and is able to play with the toy? If you give it to the child and he or she shows no interest, do not force the issue, however much you are eager to see signs of normality, precocity, or genius. You follow the leads the child provides; you do not impose your wants on those of the child."

I have seen parents so eager to see or produce signs of advancement in their preschool child, especially in regard to letter or word recognition (and reading), that they bring about the opposite of what they intended. I have seen other parents who were surprised to observe that their child had already learned certain letters and words before what one expects of children that age and, as a result, they take actions to further stimulate and reinforce what appears to be an interest, a "wanting," with very productive consequences. I am in no way suggesting, of course, that parents refrain from "testing" for the presence and strength of a child's desire to learn this or that. What I am asserting is that there is a difference between testing and foisting, between leading and imposing. Children have very short-term goals, parents have long-term goals. The artistry of parenting and teaching is how to capitalize on the short term as a step on the road to achieving long-term goals. That achievement cannot be programmed according to calendar time. What a child is interested in and wants to learn cannot be assumed to be what a parent is interested in and wants to perceive in his or her child. Parenting and teaching are very complicated affairs requiring patience, sensitive observations, creativity, and knowledge of the fact and implications of individuality: its sources, courses, and vicissitudes. In most of human history parenting and teaching were regarded as simple affairs. If it is no longer regarded as simple, it is not because the basic features of the human organism have changed but rather that the social world has dramatically changed, i.e., its values, expectations, requirements, goals, and more. The gulf between present and past conceptions of what people are and can become is like the gulf between a horse-drawn cart and a rocketing spaceship. If the concepts of individuality and productive learning today occupy our attention, it is not because of recondite theorizing by philosophers and psychologists intent on changing the world. On the contrary, they occupy our attention precisely because a changed social world will not allow us to ignore those conceptions and their practical significances.

One more example from the preschool years. No one will deny that the preschool child is a question-asking character. But that statement—as in the case of our saying that a child has learned to walk—is true, incomplete, and misleading. Before a child has learned to talk and is able verbally to articulate a question, he or she is "asking" questions, not by words but by facial expression or other body language suggestive of puzzlement, frustration, and the like. Let us take, for example, stranger anxiety. Beginning approximately around 9 months of age most children will show signs of anxiety in the presence of a stranger, especially if that stranger approaches and picks up the child. Some children will become tense and rigid, others will begin to cry and seek to return to the parent. When we say anxiety we refer to an obvious troubled state. But if you know the child—as in the case of our daughter Julie who had a strong stranger anxiety—you may see before the anxiety becomes impossible to ignore that the child has a quizzical, frowning, troubled expression that I have termed the "Who the hell are you? What are your intentions?" look. What I am saying is that even before the child is able to verbalize a question, that child can experience the question-asking stance.

Among preschoolers who are able to talk there is wide variation in the number and type of questions they ask. Some children send their parents up the wall with a seemingly constant barrage of questions. Other children ask far fewer questions. We have hardly studied and understand that variation. My observations suggest that among the different factors that can play a role, three are clearly important. First, the child does not feel that the answers he or she has been given are satisfactory or understandable, and so the child poses new questions in new ways in the hope that an understandable answer will be forthcoming. Second, the answer the child has been given is satisfactory but only for a short time, i.e., until mulling over the answer produces new questions in accord with the maxim that the more you know the more you need or want to know. Third, the child comes to feel that the adults regard his or her questions as frivolous, laughable, and of no importance; that child asks very few questions. Why ask questions that elicit silence or ridicule in others?

Question asking is the preschooler's way of dealing with the awe, wonder, and curiosity with which he or she views self, others, and the world. Freud said that dreams are the royal road to understanding the unconscious. Question asking is the royal road to understanding the preschooler and every other human being. You cannot stop posing questions to your silent self. You can be stopped from addressing other than a few questions to others. In a context of productive learning—a context that is always personal-social— questions are literally the food for thought. But that food cannot be put on the table where another crucial ingredient is missing: the feeling of trust, the feeling that when you articulate what is in your head, it will be responded to with respect, it will not be perceived as an annoyance or an interference.

Contexts for productive learning are those that stimulate, support, and sustain a child's interests, questions, and exploratory actions. That requires of adults a degree and quality of observation and reaction that, at best, we can only approximate, and there are adults who seem deaf, dumb, and blind in that regard. That is not deliberate on their part but a reflection of and ignorance about what children are, i.e., how they inevitably struggle to make sense of a puzzling, expanding social world over which they have little or no control but in regard to which they seek to be competent. We are not born with a feeling of competence, it is a hard-won feeling that, for the young child, is never fully won, an assertion that is no less true for adults, although they have "learned" to hide the incompleteness of their victory from others and too often from themselves. Contexts for productive learning are *moral* in that the adult not only assumes the obligation to understand and respect where a child is but to guide that child to where the adult thinks a child should be going and why. Between understanding and respecting, on the one hand, and guiding and leading, on the other hand, is a social–psychological terrain strewn with obstacles and opportunities, predictable and unpredictable. Productive learning is not a cut and dried affair for which there is a how-to manual, a lesson plan to which the child is expected to conform.

I said earlier that one of the ingredients of the context for productive learning is to stimulate the child. Let me give an example. I accompanied a young couple and their 4-year-old son on a trip from New Haven to New York. Once we got on the Merritt Parkway, the father announced, "I am going to count every bridge (overpass) we drive under." The following conversation ensued:

CHILD: Why do you want to do that?
FATHER: Because someone told me that every bridge is different from all the others, and there is a lot of bridges.
CHILD: You don't believe that?
FATHER: I'm not sure. That's what I want to check on. Why would they want to make each bridge different from all the others?
CHILD: I don't know. Do you?
FATHER: Well, if I had to build a lot of bridges over this parkway, I wouldn't want them to be exactly alike. That's boring. Besides, it's a long trip to New York, and it would be more interesting to drivers if each bridge was different.
CHILD: Will you slow up when we come to a bridge so I can see what is different about it? You drive too fast.
FATHER: Sure. I didn't know if you would be interested.
CHILD: I am.

A long trip became longer. The fact is that throughout the trip the parents exclaimed about many things, ranging from "It must be spring because the trees are beginning to have leaves" to "I didn't realize how many birch trees died and had to be cut down because they got a disease." The child did not respond to all such observations but to a few that obviously mystified him in some way, as his questions indicated. I cannot say, of course, what the child "learned" on that trip, but I am not going out on a limb in saying that how the child saw the world was quite different from that of a child who slept through the trip or whose parents engaged in conversation of no possible interest to the child. What my friends did was quite deliberate but was not intrusive, it did not require that the child respond. They were, so to speak, fishing, i.e., their remarks were akin to bait, a way of seeing what "hooked" the child. If I could not say what the child learned, I knew I had learned something.

I have said that in the context of productive learning it is the obligation of the adult to determine "where the child is." That is easier said than done. You may know precisely where the child is, but you do not know how and when to capitalize on that knowledge. Let us take this extreme example. You have put your 3- or 4-year-old to bed. Not long after the child is asleep you hear the child screaming, yelling. You run into the room, and it is obvious that the screaming sobbing child is in terror. You pick up the child and try to quiet and soothe him or her. The child tells you that there is a bear in the room. What do you say to the child? There was and is no bear in the room? That response will likely have the unintended effect of convincing the child that you have no comprehension of the reality he or she saw, that you are no source of comfort or even trust. Never confuse your objectivity with the reality of his or her subjectivity. If you start with where the child is, you could say that you will look under the bed, in the closet, and do that in every other room to make sure that the bear is no longer in the house. Furthermore, you will stay with and guard the child until he or she falls back to sleep. How do you productively exploit the experience for the child? You could begin the next morning by telling the child how upset you were by the child's state of terror. Of course you know the child saw the bear, but did the child know that we, everybody, sees things in sleep that seem real but not real in the sense that what we see as real when we are awake is really real? That when we are asleep our minds continue to work and we call that dreaming so that our minds fool us into believing that what we are dreaming is real? It is not my purpose here to present a script that, if followed, will have all of its intended consequences. It is not all that simple. My purpose rather is to emphasize that determining where a child is is one problem, and capitalizing on it is another one. The former does not necessarily tell you how to deal with the latter. Educators are used to hearing that they should teach children, not subject matter, a caveat intended to mean that you adapt subject matter—its substance and timing—to where you think children are: their interest, readiness, and style of comprehending. Subject matter *is* important but in order for it to become part of the child's psychological bloodstream, for the child "to own it," requires that you know where the child is, wants to go, and why. That is why parenting is such a demanding, iffy obligation, why it is that as parents we frequently fall short of the mark. A student in one of my graduate seminars once said, "You make rearing a child a scary affair in which kids can easily be scarred." I told him that children are very resilient characters who are not likely to be scarred by occasional parental lapses. It is when insensitivity to where the child is is the rule rather than the exception that productive learning is conspicuous by its absence.

The examples I have presented concerned the preschool child. That was deliberate because I wanted to emphasize the truly obvious fact that the child who starts formal schooling is not an empty vessel possessed of none or few of the assets necessary for productive learning. Granted that children will vary in the quantity and quality of those assets, the fact remains that it is the rare child who does not start school with the expectation that he or she is entering a new world that will be replete with opportunities permitting pleasure and satisfaction from new experiences, from a "growing up" that will center around new skills, new knowledge, and a sense of competence. The child expects to be taught, helped, stimulated, and changed. The child does *not* expect that most of what goes on in his or her head and life— thoughts, feelings, questions, hopes, desires, fears—will have to remain private, off limits in the social world of the classroom. The child does *not* expect that school will be a place where conformity to the procedures, goals, and values of an adult is at the expense of the sense of individuality, of being "me" and not someone else. The child is not a radical. The child wants and expects to conform. That we can count on. What the child did not count on is that the conformity will require him or her to erect a wall between the personal and the impersonal, between what one thinks and what one says, between what one says and what one is expected to say, between what is permissible to feel and articulate and what is impermissible and unsafe, between what "I feel and know I am" and what "I am expected to feel and be." Why is it that as students move from elementary to middle to high school most of them regard the classroom as boring and uninteresting places? Why is that in the classroom they appear passive (if not somnolent), uninvolved, and "going through the motions," whereas in the hallways, playground, and away from school they are alive, active, and obviously purposeful? Why is it that so many students do not feel that teachers know them? Why do so many teachers, especially those in middle and high schools, complain that motivating students is like pulling teeth?

These are not questions explainable by genes or conceptions of original sin or the orneriness to be expected in the passage from childhood to adolescence to young adulthood. That is not to say they are questions that have simple answers. But it is to say that a large part of the answer is in contexts of learning that lack almost every ingredient of productive learning.

If I had any doubts that the written word is far from adequate to convey ideas and the compelling concreteness of what our eyes and ears tell us, they were dispelled last night when I saw the movie *Mr. Holland's Opus*. I can assure the reader that I did not go to see the movie because I had reason to believe that it was relevant to what I was writing. I went to see it in part because I needed a respite from the struggle to convey through the written word what I meant by productive learning and why it was the central issue determining how schools should be governed and why. The movie says, shows, it all. For one thing, the movie captures the self-defeating features of contexts of nonproductive, classroom learning, features all too evident in schools generally and high schools particularly. For another thing, in a non-contrived way it shows how Mr. Holland, a music teacher, is driven out of sheer desperation, frustration, and utter failure to the insight that he had totally ignored the interests, ideas, and feelings of his students. Third, there was nothing and nobody in the school to help Mr. Holland gain that insight. Fourth, gaining and acting on that insight brought him into conflict with the authorities in the school and school system. Fifth, despite irrefutable evidence that students had, so to speak, awakened and were no longer sullen, bored, and recalcitrant but rather alive, motivated, and productive, Mr. Holland and his program were terminated. It is as if the point of the movie is that no good deed goes unpunished.

Albert Shanker, President of the American Federation of Teachers, must have seen the movie the week I did, because in his column in the Sunday *New York Times* for January 28, 1996, he devotes the column to Mr. Holland. With his permission I quote the last half of the column.

> But Holland has absolutely no idea what the job is. He woodenly stands with textbook in hand, asking such questions as "Who can tell me what music is?" When he is met with silence and blank faces, he continues, "O.K., nobody here knows. Turn to page 28 in your textbook. There's a definition of music there." Then he reads it.
>
> Indifference turns into desperation in Holland's classroom, but it's not the students'; it's his desperation to figure out how to teach. The movie shows the awful isolation of the green teacher. There's no "how to" manual, nobody around to help; it's sink or swim behind closed doors. Holland's struggle to learn is a seat-of-the-pants, trial-and-error, intuitive process; the movie has it right that a teacher who is going to be any good is constantly groping for ways to improve. Holland has decent instincts—

wearing a jacket and tie, he establishes decorum, explaining that he will call students Mr. or Miss So and So and they will call him Mr. Holland. But he can't seem to get anything more than order out of his class. Until one day, on the edge of panic, he turns to the piano that has been sitting unused and plays a theme from a pop song the students all know. "Who wrote this?" They snicker. "Johann Sebastian Bach." Jaws drop. But it's Holland who has made the breakthrough. He's learned that knowing your subject is essential, but it isn't enough to make you a teacher.

We watch him become increasingly skilled at connecting what he knows, loves, and is able to do with the world of his students. He teaches to the whole class and expects everyone to "get it," but he also figures out ways to reach students individually. Like many teachers, he also starts taking on lots of additional responsibilities—tutoring after school, building the school orchestra, starting a marching band, directing the annual student musical. Mr. Holland, in fact, has become a teacher and a very able one.

"Mr. Holland's Opus" is good on a lot of things about teaching. It suggests how physically grueling and emotionally demanding the work is; how great a commitment of time and self is required; where the motivation to teach comes from (love, not money); and how odd and unexpected gifts, and more than a little courage, can make an ordinary person an extraordinary teacher.

The movie is also an impassioned demonstration that art and music are not educational frills. They are academically sound ways to engage young people in learning, some of them kids who may not be reachable in any other way. But at Holland's school, the budget ax spares football, not art and music. This is happening all across the nation. I agree with Glenn Holland that it is ridiculous to suggest that the arts and music—primary means of transmitting human culture throughout history—are not among education's "basics." Without culture, he cries, students eventually will have "nothing to read or calculate." Right.

With few exceptions I have usually agreed with Mr. Shanker. Over the years his column has been an oasis of sanity and realism in the mass media. In regard to what he says about the film my agreement is total, especially what he says about transmitting via the arts human culture throughout history. But in his column Mr. Shanker does not go far enough. (He was writing a column, not a book.) So, for example, he does not say, but I assume he knows well, that Mr. Holland's college or university preparatory program was blatantly deficient in regard to orienting him to conceptions of and pedagogy for productive learning. *Those programs are part of the system.* Also, Mr. Shanker's column describes the school as a place in which teachers are unrelated to each other, unable or unwilling to learn with and from each other, and allergic to new ideas and actions. Why is this the norm in the school culture? Why are contexts for productive learning so rare for teachers? Why is it as hard and rare to "awaken" teachers as it was for Mr. Holland to arouse his students? Are we to be content with a sink or swim stance that guarantees that the Mr. Hollands of this world will be the exception rather than the rule? And, finally, the decision to terminate Mr. Holland and his program was made by a board of education that is an agent of the state and, therefore, reflective of a scale of values held by the state department of education, the legislative, and the executive branch of government. *They are parts of the system in regard to standards, priorities, and funding.* They are parts whose priorities and decisions influence not only a school and a school system but preparatory programs as well, i.e., these programs are not autonomous in the sense that colleges can devise any program they want. To be "credentialed" these programs must be approved by state agencies. And that approval rests on considerations of the purposes of schooling. But not all purposes are of equal importance. The "system" has a ready answer: learning to read and write, to learn and to manipulate arithmetic–mathematical concepts, to be knowledgeable about history, science, and literature. That is an answer in terms of subject matter, but it is a woefully inadequate and superficial answer, and for two reasons. First, it can in no way address the question why so many students are not interested in the subject matter, do not or hardly at all absorb it, and most students hardly remember it, even though they "passed the tests." Second, the answer completely glosses over what I regard as the most basic purpose of schooling: to *want* to learn more about self, others, and the world. It was bitter experience that forced Mr. Holland to see that students could be interested in subject matter if he made that subject matter have meaning, personal meaning, for them. Subject matter is important; it can be a means to the expansion of one's understanding of what the human mind has done, created, or accomplished over the millennia. But that expansion is not possible unless the student wants to learn because it has personal and instrumental value; it is not encapsulated, impersonal, undigested subject matter foisted on the student for reasons incomprehensible to the student. Schooling is not for the purpose of fine tuning rote memory. The artistry of teaching inheres in helping the student see and forge connections between what he knows and has experienced, on the one hand, and a world of knowledge and experience he or she does not and must know, on the other hand. "See and forge connections"—*the initial question is not how to do it but why you should take it seriously.* Put in another way, do you think that what I have described as contexts of productive learning—descriptions and analyses made by many people before I was born—is a feature of the modal American classroom? If you think it is not, do you think its absence is unrelated to, or plays a minor role, in the inadequacies of our system of education? Why is it that in the literally countless times I have discussed the issues with educators, parents, members of boards of education, legislators, professional people of all sorts, and students, they (with rare exceptions) agree with what I say as if not to agree is to be for sin and against virtue? And why is it that these same people will also agree that in their school days they rarely experienced contexts of productive learning and, yet, they cannot use their educational pasts in judging education today? They may criticize schools on any number of grounds, but rarely do those criticisms focus on the differences between productive and unproductive learning, between *having* to learn and *wanting* to learn, between student involvement and student disengagement. Indeed, what I say people regard as glimpses of the obvious, as indeed they are. But why is it so difficult to take the obvious seriously? The answer is a very complicated one but I offer the opinion that the most potent reason is that intuitively people know that if you take productive learning seriously, the existing educational system will have to be scrapped, not reformed or restructured, but scrapped. So they, as I long did, shy away from a conclusion that leads to possible actions and futures that are murky, cloudy, and fraught with many uncertainties. It is as if they would rather deal with a self-defeating present rather than engage a future that does not contain certainties. That is why I regard the constitutional convention of 1787 one of the historic chapters in human history: It said "no more" to the Articles of Confederation and proceeded to develop a document that would harmonize power, individuality, and individual freedom. They did not do this with any strong feeling of certainty, without fear that the document would not achieve its intended purposes, without questions about the ability and willingness of a largely uneducated people to abide by the letter and spirit of the new document. They did what they felt they had to do if the goal was to forge a nation.

In the chapters that follow I shall sketch, discuss, and justify a system of educational governance that will have as its primary function creating and sustaining contexts of productive learning. I shall not be concerned with the way things are but with how they can and should be. I entreat the reader to adopt a similar stance because I assume that some readers will regard what I say as impractical, even though many of the same readers know in their heart of hearts that the existing system is glaringly impractical. Some will regard what I say as visionary in a pejorative sense, i.e., an indulgence of wish-fulfilling fantasy that has the sole virtue of escaping from the real world. That was precisely the same argument offered in regard to ending slavery, giving the vote to women, opening the doors of the workplace to women, electing a Catholic president, enacting Social Security legislation, and more. It is not only an argument against thinking and using one's imagination. I am reminded here of the joke about two friends who meet and friend A says "This is the best of all possible worlds." To which friend B replies, "I am afraid you are right." This is not the best of all possible worlds, and it is our moral obligation to suggest or help bring about changes we hope will, by the verdicts of history, be viewed favorably. Posterity is the cruelest of critics, and I have no doubt that in regard to our educational system posterity will regard our feckless tinkering in the most negative terms.

CHAPTER IV

The Governors:
Teachers and Parents

I start with the elementary school years because they pose all of the important issues about the relationships between governance and productive learning in the later school years. Those relationships are not determined by the age of the student. They are required on the basis of an agreement about an overarching purpose, an understanding, and a value judgment. The purpose is to sustain, reinforce, and support students' wanting to do and learn more. The understanding is that the purpose cannot be achieved unless students perceive that learning is in some important ways meaningful and necessary for what they are and want to become. The value judgment is that it is a "good," a moral obligation, so to expand students' knowledge of self, others, and the world that they increasingly feel more competent to make choices that living does and will present to them; they are choices that should always take into account the knowledge, opinions, values, and experience of others. Choices are not exercises in narcissism or reflections of mindless permissiveness. If adults "owe" something to children, we also want children to feel they owe something to adults as well as to other students.

What do we want a teacher to know about a child? How might a teacher go about acquiring that knowledge? Consistent with what we know about productive learning we take for granted that a teacher will want to know "where the child is" and "where he or she is coming from." And we take it for granted that parents will want to provide whatever relevant knowledge they have, if appropriately and sensitively asked. Such knowledge is obviously important in the case of children starting school for the first time. Because that knowledge is sought in order to be maximally helpful to student, teacher, and parents—especially to the teacher who wants seriously to take account of a child's individuality—this question arises: When should that knowledge be sought? The answer is *not* after the child has started school but *before* he or she has started school. And the answer explicitly assumes that that initial meeting establishes a relationship between teacher and parent that makes it easy for both to arrange subsequent meetings whenever each of them thinks a meeting would be helpful. Parents are resources to teachers and vice versa. For a teacher to regard meeting with a parent as a form of noblesse obligé guarantees estrangement and the censorship of thought and feeling. As soon as a parent feels that he or she is being "talked down to," that parent will regard the teacher as the child is likely to regard the teacher who sees that child as an unformed vessel who has no sense of identity or individuality. The parent is part of the context of productive learning.

I am sure that many readers are asking themselves several questions. "Does he realize how much time it would take it for a teacher to see each parent before a child starts school? And how much time it would take to meet with each parent, say, several times or more during the year? How many teachers would be willing to spend a good part of the month of August meeting with parents? Who would pay the teachers for that extra time, which will not be minuscule? And when do we see working parents? At night? On weekends?"

These are legitimate questions, but they miss the point I made earlier. If you agree with and take seriously what I have said about contexts of productive learning, then what I have said about parent–teacher meetings (in the case of children beginning schooling) is not only important but a necessity. It is not a frill, an empty ritual, or play acting. Of course teachers should be paid for their time. And, again of course, teachers should, within reasonable limits, be flexible in regard to working parents. Teachers should not be expected to be philanthropists but neither should they regard themselves as exempt from the professional obligation to try to accommodate to the life conditions of others. If you are a professional, you have something to profess, a something that is both substantive, ethical, and moral.

What does this have to do with governance? It means that the community and the legislative and executive branches of government—who collect and spend taxes—would be obliged to regard the funding not as a gift or bribe but as a necessary way of supporting productive learning. We hear much from these sectors about the bedrock importance of parent involvement, and what I have advocated is *one* way of demonstrating how seriously that involvement should be taken. When a governor calls a special session of the legislature, those legislators are paid for their time. That is taken for granted. Similarly, if you require teachers to give more and special time to discharging an agreed-upon responsibility, the system should make that possible. But that will only be possible if the policy makers and funders are crystal clear about the overarching purpose of schooling. It would also be the obligation of the funding sources to pass legislation that would allow working parents to be released from work for a half day x number of times during the school year to attend meetings with teachers regardless of whether it is the parent or teacher who seeks the meeting. Nothing would be deducted from the parents' pay. Just as teachers and others have paid days of personal leave, so should working parents be able to meet with teachers without penalties when necessary. I said "x number of times" because I do not want to be bogged down in trying to decide on whether it should be 3, 5, or 7 days. In this case the devil is not in the details but in the principle. Once the principle is accepted numbers will not be a thorny obstacle.

But there is another aspect to what I have proposed that is not concerned with time and money but is no less important, and I would argue that in some ultimate sense will be more important. The purpose of the parent–teacher meetings is not only to share information or as a vehicle for getting to know each other but to define accountability. No longer will teachers be *solely* responsible for the educational–intellectual development of students. Parents and teachers will be jointly responsible by which I mean that parents, no less than teachers, have obligations to understand and take seriously what they can and should do at home to support the concept of productive learning. The context of family can be congruent with or in opposition to productive learning. Allowing a child to watch TV for hours on end is doing the child no favor. And that is true if no one reads to the child, or tells him or her no stories, or does not elicit or respond to a child's questions, or does not provide the child with toys that sustain his or her interest, or shows no interest in what the child is doing and experiencing in school, or never or rarely takes him or her to community sites or happenings that would stimulate the child's interests and curiosities. Just as parents will hold teachers accountable for what goes on in the classroom, teachers will hold parents accountable for the quality and context of learning in the home. Aside from meeting and discussing these matters with parents, the school will be required to provide parents with a brochure containing, among other things I will take up shortly, the responsibilities of parents and teachers for the education of their children.

What about parents who are poor, uneducated, and may not even be able to read? Are those features to which educators are expected to be sensitive but to which they are not expected to take some concrete actions? On what moral and pedagogical grounds can one justify inaction in regard to features that negatively affect learning, directly or indirectly or both? At the very least, each school should have a fund that is used to purchase age-appropriate books and toys that are then given and owned by child and family. It would also be the responsibility of the school to be of whatever help is realistically possible in regard to why and how those materials might be employed. Here, again, the objection will be made that another time-consuming task is being given to the school. And some would object to what appears be an intrusion by the school into family life. The first objection implicitly concedes the point: what I recommend is desirable and should be put into practice, but it is impractical and self-defeating. The objection is valid only if one is judging on the basis of how schools are *now* organized, funded, and function. As they now are, schools cannot regard my proposal as other than utopian musings that have the virtue of allowing one to escape from reality. It is one things to escape from reality—to leave it alone, so to speak—it is quite another thing to take it seriously enough to seek to change it. I must also remind the reader that one of the conclusions derived from the long history of the literature on utopias is that over time many aspects of those publications became standard in what later became quotidian reality. The constitution of 1787 was regarded by many, here and abroad, as a utopian document.

     The second objection is on the grounds of the protection of privacy and parental authority against the "big brother," freedom-constraining stance. I said earlier that parents will be given a brochure spelling out the rights and responsibilities of teachers and parents, i.e., the constitution of the school. I then went on to say that teachers will provide some parents with books and toys that they will be helped to use in productive ways with their children. And so we come to the heart of the matter: the political principle, which is that if you are going to be affected by a policy, decision, or practice you should stand in some relationship to the formulation and implementation of any or all of them. Concretely, whatever I have said (or will say) assumes that parents and teachers, in equal numbers, will decide the substance, purpose, and means of implementation of educational policy. *The political principle is not only about rights but about accountability.* Parents, no less than teachers, are accountable for the development of children. Whether and to what degree a school achieves its intended, agreed-on purposes no longer should praise or blame be directed to one source, i.e., educators. Just as war should not be left to the generals, education is too encompassing and important a task to be left to educators; it is not a task educators have ever or could ever or should have been allowed to be their sole responsibility. If it takes a village to raise a child, it takes more than teachers to educate a child.

There are two reasons for my position: the requirements of the political principle, and its consequences for clarifying accountability. That, I should hasten to add, does not guarantee that the overarching purpose of schooling will be achieved in part or in whole. What the requirements and consequences of the political principle make possible is that there will be a forum in which the issues surrounding productive learning can be discussed, debated, and decided. How well those issues will be clarified and implemented cannot be legislated. What can be legislated, and explicitly so, is why that forum exists. It exists to decide a variety of problems and purposes, but none of them is as important as creating and supporting contexts of productive learning. The forum is not one created and shaped by individuals or agencies outside that school. It is a forum, essentially a governing body, indigenous to that school.[1] It is responsible for preparing a school budget, allocating resources, selecting teachers, developing supportive constituencies, and instituting procedures the purpose of which is to provide data that are the basis for self-correcting actions, and to deal with any other question, issue, and problem bearing on productive learning. These are awesome, difficult responsibilities and tasks, I know. But if those tasks and responsibilities are not in the province of such a governing body, they will be put in the province of others who are "elsewhere" and who are relatively unknowledgeable about *that* school: its demography, its culture, its students, its parents, its teachers, and its resources (actual and potential). That kind of ignorance and insensitivity guarantee that the individuality of that school, like the individuality of the student, will succumb to the creativity-destroying requirement of uniformity. The "absentee landlord," by virtue of his or her interpersonal and geographical distance, cannot engender the quantity and quality of commitment crucial to achieving and sustaining contexts of productive learning. I am not describing the absentee landlord as a villain but rather taking seriously what I consider to be a glimpse of the obvious.

For a group to achieve an agreed-on goal requires at the least the commitment of those who, in a most personal and intimate psychological sense, own the problem. When that sense of ownership is absent or weak, accountability goes by the boards. It is balkanized, no one is truly accountable. In earlier pages I emphasized that in the classroom the context of productive learning is one that engenders and sustains a willing commitment to learning, i.e., not because it is required by others but because that commitment comes from within the individual. That is the compelling point of the movie *Mr. Holland's Opus.* As long as Mr. Holland required of his students a commitment they were not able or prepared to give because it literally made no sense to them—the students and Mr. Holland were strangers if not enemies to each other—the classroom was a stifling, joyless, impersonal, boring, hostile affair by no means unusual in high school classrooms. When he finally acted on the insight that requiring commitment was one thing and eliciting it quite another thing, productive learning could occur. Commitment did not require legislation, it was willingly given. Similarly, to the extent that the governing board of the school willingly assumes the responsibility to act consistent with the overarching purposing of schooling because it is *their* task and obligation, not a task and obligation imposed on them, the goals of productive learning stand a chance of being realized. And when I say "stands a chance," I mean just that. Good intentions are necessary but not sufficient conditions for achieving purposes. Not in the crucible of human affairs.

There are several objections (to put it mildly?) to what I have proposed, but two require reply at this point because they are interrelated. The first would take the following form: "What do parents know about schools, teachers, teaching, curricula, budgeting, assessment, and more? You are being irresponsible when you advocate giving parents an equal status with educators in matters for which parents are not even amateurs. You say that a professional is one who has something to profess based on preparation, personal experience, and the experience of other professionals. On what basis do parents have something to profess? Are we to give what they profess the same status as that which we profess? You are always quoting Mencken's caveat that for every social problem there is a simple answer that is wrong. Your proposal confirms Mencken's wise remark. It is as if you want to appear as the super democrat for whom obvious distinctions among people do not exist, or can be easily overcome or erased. Come off it, Professor Sarason, you have been in the halls of ivy too long. If you once thought you knew schools, you certainly do not know them now."

Let me begin my defense by saying that since I retired in 1989 I probably have been in more classrooms in more schools, I have talked to and with more teachers, I have read more articles and books about or by teachers than almost all of my objectors. Having said that, I can assure my objectors that I know that in and of itself experience does not automatically confer validity on whatever conclusions I have drawn or proposals I have advocated. *That, I must emphasize, holds no less for my objectors than it does for me. That is not an argumentum ad hominem.* Between experience and conclusions is a minefield of traps with such labels as wish fulfillment, illogic, imprisoning habit, blinding partisanship, and selective perception and attention. I take it for granted that the human mind is a fascinating amalgam of assets and deficits. Therefore, I cannot cavalierly dismiss objections to what I have said (and will say in this and later chapters). By the same token I ask that what I say be given a hearing, however strange, disturbing, and unfamiliar it may be. I must remind the reader that the purpose of this book is to start a discussion about the inadequacies of our schools. If you hold the belief that, generally speaking, our schools are achieving their purposes as those purposes are currently proclaimed both by educators and the public, I see no point in your continuing to read this book. And if you hold the belief that, again generally speaking, our schools, especially our urban schools, are improving or can be improved without radically changing the system, this is not a book for you. This is a book for those, by no means small in number, who are wrestling with the question: Why in the post–World War II era, after spending scores of billions of dollars, can few people generate any optimism that the public schools can be improved, and find themselves looking with favor (or with far less skepticism) on diverse efforts—ranging from vouchers to charter schools to privatization—that directly attack the system qua system?

Let me now give parts of my answer.[2]

1. The substance of the objections is in every respect identical to that which was raised by many people (in the convention of 1787 and during the ratification process) against the constitution. Were people up to the responsibilities and power that were going to be accorded them? Could you trust the masses to be wise and to resist fads, fashions, and the blandishments of self-serving, power-seeking scoundrels? Could you entrust the fate of a nation to the ordinary citizen, whose passions and unsophistication would overwhelm what was in the best interests of the larger collectivity? Did we want mob rule? If the constitution had the substance it did and obtained the ratification sought, it was with prayer and hope as well as the realization that the blatant inadequacies of the Articles of Confederation required a new direction, albeit one that had its risks. I do not point this out as a way of saying, "Look, they did it, they placed their faith in people, so why object to what I have proposed?" I point this out to my objectors only to remind them that *their argument is not self-evidently valid,* historically, morally, and conceptually. Are there risks? Of course. Is what we have now demonstrably inadequate? Of course.

2. The objections, again, are identical to those voiced by many educational administrators, legislators, and boards of educations against giving *teachers* the authority and responsibility to determine educational purposes, priorities, and use of resources. Teachers, they say, are unsophisticated in matters of administration, law, finance, and budgets. They are unprepared for this new authority and responsibility, and on what basis should one expect they can become competent in these matters? What you are proposing is that we go from the frying pan into the fire. No, thank you. And to compound this felony in misguided thinking, you want teachers to share this authority and responsibility with parents who are even more ignorant and unsophisticated than teachers! Someone said that it is hard to be completely wrong and that is true here. Suffice it to say here, the question is not what teachers now can do but what they can learn to do, and how quickly. The self-fulfilling prophecy

can work in one of two ways. One way assumes than an individual or a group cannot learn something and/or be trusted with this or that responsibility, you act toward them in accord with that assumption, and you end up proving that assumption, unaware that your initial, untested assumption already contained the "final" proof. The other way is that you assume that the individual or group can learn, you act in ways consistent with that assumption, and you are not surprised if, more often than not, your initial expectations are realized. In my experience, at least, the first way produces far fewer surprises than the second way. For example, the modal American classroom is not comprehensible apart from the unverbalized assumption that students cannot be trusted to govern themselves, to learn with and from other students in small, semi-autonomous groups, or play a meaningful role in determining the constitution of the classroom, i.e., the rules, regulations, and values governing social relationships and learning. It is as if students require taming and socialization, otherwise they would run amok. There can only be one source of control, power, and direction. The teacher, and only the teacher knows best. The "good" student is one who conforms, one who is unformed and needs to be formed, in much the same way that Professor Higgins shaped Liza Doolittle in *Pygmalion* and in its musical play and movie version, *My Fair Lady*. I said the "modal classroom" because there are classrooms, albeit clearly in the minority, governed by dramatically opposite assumptions and where anarchy, turbulence, volatility, or passive conformity are not in evidence. Assumptions are just that: assumptions about what people are and how they should and need to be managed. Assumptions are not empirical facts, however much we lull ourselves into believing they are factual.

3. My proposal was not dreamed up in an armchair. It was stimulated by countless stories, anecdotes, frustrations, resigned musings, and the articulated personal perspectives of a large number of teachers and administrators. If these were sources of stimulation to my thinking, congruent with what I personally observed, the fact is that no one came up with alternatives to the way things are. If they agreed on anything, it was that there was nothing basically wrong with the system that an infusion of better and wiser people would not remedy. The possibility that it was far more the system than the personal attributes of those in it that made the current situation what it is was never considered. And, I should add, no one asked of themselves: How did it happen that the enthusiasm and idealism with which I entered the profession so quickly got diluted, if not extinguished? Why do so many of my colleagues feel the same way?

Let us return to the objection to giving teachers (and parents) authority and power in all educational decisions. I return to this objection because it ignores two facts, one is indisputably obvious and the other too frequently masked and too gingerly discussed. The first fact is that what we call the educational system includes colleges and universities that have preparatory programs for educators. When the state legislature, another part of the system, passes legislation that changes directly or indirectly the requirements for becoming a teacher, or the responsibilities of teachers, or the intellectual mix of students a teacher should be expected to teach, or the number of postgraduate courses a teacher must take, or the legal and ethical responsibilities a teacher must assume in regard to students and parents—when that kind of legislation is enacted, colleges and universities are expected, if not required, to provide the appropriate courses and experiences. They screen, prepare, and for all practical purposes credential educators. When legislation to improve teaching and educational outcomes is enacted, the state department of education is given the task of spelling out what that means for preparatory programs as well as determining if and how those guidelines are implemented in ways consistent with legislative intent. I point out these glimpses of the obvious because in the literature on educational reform the words *systemic reform* appear with great frequency but the word systemic does not refer to such major parts of the system as the legislative, the state department of education, and the preparatory programs in colleges and universities. That narrow conception of systemic has several consequences. The general public is not helped to comprehend the parts of the system and the nature of their relationships. It fosters the unwarranted belief that schools can be changed, and those changes can be sustained, regardless of what happens elsewhere in the system. And, most fatefully, it diverts attention away from examining how these other parts should be changed if they are to be truly supportive of school change rather than being obstacles to change. If we have learned anything about changing a school—let alone a school district—it can be put in three statements.

1. The attempt to change a school is an endlessly complicated, frustrating, draining affair. And if you add to that what is required to sustain the change, it is no wonder that reformers experience burnout.
2. Most reform efforts hardly get off the ground. A fair number that do get started get aborted before any change has occurred. With rare exceptions those that endure fall short of their goals.
3. Neither the school district, the legislature, the state department of education, or colleges and universities see it as their primary obligation to support and sustain school change. They, of course, rhetorically proclaim otherwise, but the brute fact is that their philosophy, priorities, and organizational style make a mockery of that rhetoric. The current system is a balkanized one containing no features of a self-correcting system; it learns little or nothing from experience. It is as if the system was developed to be unproductive.

I have had the opportunity to be able to make extensive observations over a period of years of two efforts to change a school (Trubowitz et al., 1984, 1997; Heckman, 1995). Despite points 1, 2, and 3, I regard these efforts as more than modestly successful. Indeed, initially I expected both efforts would fail. The stories are predictably complex and do not allow one to explain their achievement by any one factor. But if I had to scale the factors that contributed to the achievements I would give first place to the working alliance forged by teachers and parents. And in terms of sustaining the change no other factor comes close. Those judgments are amply confirmed by the descriptions, experiences, and conclusions contained in the research literature on school change.

Now to the second fact relevant to the objection of giving teachers power and authority. The long and short of it is that preparatory programs for teachers are grossly inadequate in terms of helping its would-be practitioners understand children, classrooms, schools, school systems, and the larger system in which all of this is embedded (Sarason, 1986, 1992). And by "understanding children" I mean comprehending the differences between productive and nonproductive learning, between starting with what children are and where they are, and the consequences of requiring them to conform to a preconceived mold and determining what will be learned, when, and how. If the beginning teacher has been sensitized to anything, it has been the bedrock necessity of leaving students in no doubt about who is in control of learning and who is the source of discipline. I have never met a teacher who denied that when he or she started to teach their first class their major concern was: Will I be able to control the students? Will I be an adequate and fair disciplinarian? Will they go along with me? What will I do if a student challenges my authority in some way? These questions reflect a stance resting on a psychology that views children as teacher-adult devouring animals, who will demand a mile if you give them an inch, who have no intrinsic desire to be understood, to be competent, to seek answers to questions about themselves, others, and the world around them. Their deficits are far greater than their assets; they are unformed, they need to be shaped; they can get shaped only by external others; they have to be instructed, informed, directed; they have no internal compass or sense of direction. The modal American classroom is incomprehensible apart from that kind of psychology and the pedagogy derived from it. Mr. Holland is as clear an example as you will find of what happens when you approach the classroom in these ways.

The objectors to my proposal could raise another issue: "Not only do you propose that teachers be given an unusual, if not unheard of, degree of responsibility and authority, but you also expect them to work hand-in-hand with parents who have the most superficial understanding of learning. It's not a case of the blind leading the blind but it comes awfully close to being just that." This criticism could be made by the objectors, but it has not and will not be raised because to raise it is to expose how egregiously deficient preparatory programs for teachers and administrators are in regard to what parents know or would like to know; how they perceive schools and how they see how schools perceive them; the political principle justifying and requiring their deep involvement and commitment; and why parents no less than educators should be held accountable for what schools are and how well goals are being met. Teachers view parents no differently than they view children, just as administrators view teachers, which is to say that administrators regard teachers as people whose place is in the classroom and only the classroom because beyond its borders are roles and problems about which they know little and are incapable of comprehending and confronting.

To deal and work with parents is not only a matter of technique. Technique is the overt manifestation and implementation of a rationale containing philosophical, moral, psychological, and political facets. If I had to put it in a most succinct form, it would be as follows: Technique is revealing of what you think people know and can know, what they are and can become, what your obligations are to help another person become more than what he or she is, all of this revealing of the degree to which you are aware of the difference between the positive and negative consequences of the self-fulfilling prophecy. In the realm of human affairs we have no choice about whether or not to adopt a self-fulfilling stance. We do have a choice at the same time that we have the obligation to justify that choice, never to forget that how and why we choose affects the lives of others.

Have I not, the reader may ask, rather thoroughly given my objectors justification for their position? Have I not said that teachers are not prepared for the responsibilities I propose to give them? Are the objectors right in saying that it will be a case of the blind leading the blind?

My answer is in several parts. The first is that I wanted to emphasize that preparatory programs are part of the system and that unless they change in appropriate ways the likelihood that school change will be even relatively successful (and sustained) will be somewhat above zero. Granted that current major reform efforts call for new roles and responsibilities for parents and teachers—albeit to an obviously lesser extent than in my proposal—why have the inadequacies of preparatory programs been exempt from criticism, especially since the results of these reform efforts are very far from robust? How do you justify an effort at "systemic change" and ignore preparatory programs that are indisputably part of the system? Why is so much criticism directed to schools and their personnel and practically none to the programs that select, prepare, and credential those personnel? The second part of my answer is that in the existing system accountability is so diffuse, if not chaotic, as to guarantee that no part will learn anything from any other part of the system. What we have now is the antithesis of a self-correcting system. Even worse, it is a system with no agreement on an overarching purpose, e.g., the creation and sustaining of contexts of productive learning. My proposal assumes that there should be an overarching purpose and that the commitment to it, and the implementation of it, are the responsibility of the two groups with the greatest stake in the enterprise, the two groups most immediately and personally involved, and, therefore, the groups that will be accountable, explicitly so.

The final part of my answer is that I do not regard parents and teachers as so ignorant and unknowledgeable, so lacking in the capacity to learn, so devoid of whatever is meant by wisdom and reason, so unable or unwilling to comprehend the differences between productive and unproductive learning, and so unwilling or unable to move in new directions as to be proof positive that they will make the present situation more dangerous and feckless than it now is. That does not mean that I regard teachers and parents as having more wisdom and insight than other groups, because they do not. What I am saying is that they do not have less wisdom and insight than others, and their capacity to learn is not less either. Put in another way: If parents and teachers are given and assume the roles and responsibilities explicitly and implicitly contained in my proposal, and if they are not constrained by existing rules and regulations of a failed tradition, and if they are truly free to take innovative actions that to others seem strange and risky, they stand a chance of demonstrating the crucial significances and consequences of productive learning. A reform effort not powered at all points by a conception of productive learning will have no demonstrable, percolating effects.

In my book *The Creation of Settings and the Future Societies* (1972), I emphasized and illustrated a point that is relevant here. If you ask members of a university faculty, "How do you justify the existence of a university?" the answer, with few exceptions, will be that a university is a place that creates the conditions in which its faculty can learn, change, and grow. You can have a university without students. The assumption is that by discharging its obligation to the faculty that faculty will be able to create those same conditions for students. Now, how would teachers in an elementary school justify the existence of the school? The answer is that it exists for the education of children. That is a very different answer from that given by university faculty. I would argue that an elementary school should exist both for the productive learning of teachers and students. If contexts for productive learning do not exist for teachers, those teachers cannot create and sustain those contexts for students. Those contexts do not or hardly exist for teachers. On the contrary, in the modal school teachers are in a context of discouragement.

My proposal does not assume a "Here are the keys to the kingdom" approach. What it does assume is that: (1) Parents and teachers are willing to embark on the venture; (2) They have been provided and discussed materials (written, films) illustrative of contexts of productive learning; (3) They are enabled as a group to observe such contexts; and (4) They have access to individuals who potentially can be helpful as consultants, sounding boards, and support. *In short, they are not catapulted into a sink or swim situation but rather made aware that they, no less than students, are in a context of learning the purpose of which is clear but the course of which cannot be described in a predictable, step-by-step fashion. That is not to say the course is unpredictable but rather that productive learning cannot be driven by calendar time.* Further, they have been sensitized to their obligation to develop forums and procedures that alert them to when and how the venture can be changed and improved, i.e., you can plan, plan, plan, and discuss, discuss, and discuss, but you have to be prepared for the reality that the process of creation and implementation brings to the fore issues, problems, and ambiguities ignored or glossed over. The change process is not for the fainthearted, let alone for those who paint themselves into a corner in which the admission of imperfection is a signal of defeat or failure. That is a glimpse of the obvious but the history of educational reform is a history of not taking the obvious seriously. The governance of our educational system is not one that has the overarching purpose of supporting productive learning for students and teachers, and it should occasion no surprise whatsoever that parents are not even in the picture. My proposal puts them in the picture because they are one of the two stakeholders most immediately and personally involved with and concerned for the quality and the outcomes of the enterprise, and that determines why they should be given the authority and responsibility to govern that enterprise.

Will there be some mistakes and conflicts? Of course. Will there be schools where parents and teachers are unwilling to give the time that governance will require? Of course. My proposal does not require that form of governance, it makes the opportunity possible. Legislation should require that parents who wish to be available for their role but cannot because they are working will be released from work up to x days a year without loss of pay. I expect, and they should expect, that they will be giving more than the equivalent of x days but they should also expect they should not be "paid" for time they will have to give in evenings and weekends. They are not going to be running a business but a nonprofit enterprise involving the present and future of children. Yes, I do assume that many parents will be willing to give the time, will not view it as an oppressive burden, but rather as an opportunity to enlarge their knowledge and experience, an opportunity not ordinarily available or possible in the lives of many people.

My proposal dramatically enlarges the authority and responsibility of teachers. It was not many decades ago that teachers overcame their resis-

tance to joining a union in order to have more power in matters of salary
and working conditions. On the surface it appeared they were interested only
in increasing what then was a scandalously low salary. Without in any way
denying the justice of their grievances, what the teachers sought was *respect*
for what they were and did. They did not want to be treated as peons who
did what they were told by those above them. They were "told" they had
to conform and submit, they saw others as seeing them as children who could
not understand or participate in important matters of educational policy
and procedure. If in subsequent decades their salaries have increased, it has
not been accompanied by the feeling that they are truly recognized and
respected by those above them in the system. When we say we respect someone, we mean we understand and accept what they are and think as well as
what they want to become. In the present system teachers have good reason to believe that others do not respect the capacity of teachers to be other
than what they are: someone whose work is an encapsulated classroom and
who should not and cannot be expected to take responsibility for anything
beyond that classroom. Socialized as they are in that kind of institutional
culture it should occasion no surprise that a fair number of teachers come
to esteem themselves as others esteem them. It also will not surprise me if
teachers regard my proposal as another downgrading of their status. Do you
mean, some will say, that teachers will share authority and responsibility
with parents who are not professionals? As I have pointed out in detail elsewhere (Sarason, 1995b), the spirit of that question is precisely that which
informs the stance of educational administrators in opposing giving teachers any role in matters of policy and decisions. If I expect that there will be
teachers who will not embrace my proposal, I do expect there will be far more
than a few who will, provided that two conditions are met. The first is that
their compensation will be appropriate to their new roles and its time
demands. Second, that the rules of the game will be clear that parents and
teachers will have the freedom to go their own way, and not to be watched,
supervised, and ruled by others who, however well intentioned, are not totally
involved in *that* school, and who are more concerned with uniformity among
schools than with individuality.

It was not my purpose in this chapter, as it will not be in subsequent
ones, to deal with all of the criticisms, questions, and reservations my proposal
will elicit. But there are two issues I can safely assume will have occurred to
the reader. The first has to do with giving the school control over the allocation of funds, i.e., removing control from the central office. In a document *Reinventing Central Office. A Primer for Successful Schools,* Chicago's
Cross City Campaign for Urban School Reform (1995) deals forthrightly with
that issue. The document is clear about what it needs to change:

Abolish:
- the centralized control of funds
- the central office's monopoly on services
- the present allocation formulas
- the unnecessary categorical and restricted federal and state funding rules
- the requirement to return unspent funds to central office
- the obscure and overly technical budget documents

The document then sketches the steps that can be taken and that obligate the council of the school periodically to make public how the funds were used. I found their suggestions reasonably clear, responsible, and realistic. The document is the fruit of the collaborative efforts of eight individuals whose credentials establish, at the very least, that they are people who know the current system and are not engaged in witch hunts. What is so refreshing about the publication is its unequivocal recommendation that the governance of the existing system is a self-defeating one in which accountability is diffused or masked or both. What is disappointing is the absence of a commitment to what I consider to be the overarching purpose of schooling. That is to say, the document does not address the question: Is there an overarching purpose that, if not realized, makes the realization of all other purposes unlikely, if not impossible?

Can one come up with a plan that *guarantees* that a parent–teacher governing group will expend funds in consistent, efficient, honorable ways? The answer is no and that answer would be the same if the organization was a private company, a church, or a social club, and it is certainly the answer one has to give in regard to existing school systems. To ask for a guarantee, at this time, is an effective way of distracting attention away from the task of recognizing the inadequacies and failures of the current system in creating and sustaining productive learning for students *and* teachers, and from devising a new governance system that is clear about the differences between productive and unproductive contexts of learning. If there is no clarity about that, we will continue to reinvent past wheels that turned out to be flat tires. The Chicago document is one of many indications that people in diverse sectors of the society find themselves driven to the conclusion that the existing system of governance is hopelessly unrescuable.

The second issue that will have occurred to readers can be put in the form of questions: "Let's say you have the kind of school your proposal calls for. What assurance is there that they are being consistent with the overarching purpose, and how will the larger community be able to judge that consistency and the achievement of educational goals? To whom and in what ways will it be accountable? What basis will be provided so as to allow some external agency to say 'Stop, no more,' or 'Right on,' or 'Some changes are necessary'? What self-correcting procedures will there be? Good intentions are one thing, getting to or near your goals is another thing. Will the teachers and parents be accountable only to themselves?" Those, of course, are legitimate questions, and the next chapter is an attempt by *one individual* to begin to answer them. The italicized words are a way of reminding the reader that I know that devising a new governance system should not be done in isolation but rather in a context and through a process maximizing awareness of the universe of alternatives that should be considered. As I said earlier, what is required is something akin to the constitutional convention of 1787, where its participants engaged in a competition of ideas and possibilities, where different interests were represented, where common ground could be found for seemingly opposing views, where it could become apparent that the problems being confronted and discussed did not have one, and only one, solution, where it could be acknowledged that any resolution or compromise brought risk and uncertainty in its wake. In the realm of human affairs we are never dealing with problems that have a solution the way 4 divided by 2 is a solution.

Those are the reasons I resisted writing this book. It is not about a set of problems and proposals one individual should be expected to "solve." It is not only because the problems are so complex but also because they are problems taking us over uncharted seas. I am in the same position as the kind of school I am trying to describe and justify, with the crucial difference that, unlike me, that school will have external sources of ideas, support, counsel, and evaluation. Productive learning requires, among other things, feedback. The kind of school I am proposing will not operate in a vacuum.

NOTES

[1]In a later chapter I take up how assessment of the efficacy of that forum should be done and by whom. Suffice it to say here, the assessment would be done by parents and teachers from other schools.

[2]My answer in regard to parents is given in much greater detail in my book, *Parental Involvement and the Political Principle. Why the Existing Governance Structure of Schools Should Be Abolished* (1995b).

Some Self-Correcting Features

I n the traditional classroom the student cannot avoid the conclusion that an adult, the teacher, defines learning as a process in which the learner gets the right answer by individual, and only individual, understanding and effort. And, as Wertheimer (1945) observed, the teacher expects that the right answer will be gotten in the "right way," i.e., as the teacher has previously demonstrated. When Wertheimer demonstrated an alternative way to solve the problem of determining the area of the parallelogram, the students (to Wertheimer's consternation) said he was wrong. One problem, one process, one answer, and, I should add, a solo learner. Talking to another student, seeking his or her help, or (just as bad) helping another student are frowned on and often punished. You are and should be on your own! You are competing as an individual against other individuals. What I have just described has been most thoughtfully anatomized and criticized by Arnstine (1995). The following is from his book:

> Individuality, which is the concern of education, must also be distinguished from another sense of "individual": the sense that is implied when we speak of individualism. Individualism is largely an economic term, referring to

the capacity of a single person to be self-sufficient. Individualism thus refers
to a point of view about the capacities of people. This point of view is not
empirically testable. Can people *really* manage for themselves in this complex society? What would it *mean* to be really self-sufficient? And since it
underlies a broader point of view about how an economic system ought to
work (on the basis of competitive individual entrepreneurship) it is part
of an ideology. When the terms "individual" and "individuality" are used
in the following discussion, no reference is intended to the ideology of
individualism, or individual entrepreneurship. I mean only by "individual"
a person whose education has enabled her to develop, on the basis of her
own reasoned judgments, a range of unique talents and skills.

Education, then, is concerned with individuals (this is why most events
that occur in a lecture hall *may* be informative, but cannot be educative).
As we'll see later on, the education of individuals is sometimes best carried on within groups of people. But just as the focus or aim of socialization is on the community or social group, so the focus of education is on
the individual. And because individual persons are the main concern of
educators, what must be of primary importance to educators is the quality of the experience of learners. (p. 14)

If there is anything in the research literature of the past several decades
that has been demonstrated and replicated, it is that group or cooperative
learning can be a context for productive learning. Students in small groups
can learn with and from, stimulate, and help one another. They become active
stakeholders in their learning, they are not passive recipients of facts and knowledge that so often have little or no personal significance for them in and out
of the classroom. Given the research basis for group learning, why, then, has
it been appropriately implemented in so few classrooms, even though with
each passing year more and more books and journal articles speak so approv-
ingly about the rationale for group or productive learning? That is one of
the most important questions the parent–teacher governing body will have
to address because the psychological rationale for cooperative learning is so
fundamentally different than that which has given rise to classrooms where
the teacher is the source of all knowledge, the sole determiner of what will
be learned and how. When I say that the major responsibility of the parent–teacher group is to create and sustain contexts of productive learning, I
mean that they will have to be helped to address the issue of cooperative learning, and for two reasons. One is in relation to the selection of teachers, and
the second is that they have to face the failure of college or university programs to prepare educators in the spirit and application of cooperative learning. It will also, I predict, cause them to consider how their school can and
should be used for the preparation of educators. My proposal is intended to
not only have a local effect but also a percolating one throughout a system,
the parts of which are unconnected, isolated from each other, and, unwittingly

to be sure, antagonistic to each other. It is a problem producing a system that is not self-correcting. I shall have more to say about the role of the school in preparing educators in a later chapter.

It has been pointed (e.g., Sharan & Sharan, 1992; Sharan et al., 1982) that one reason cooperative learning is so infrequent in schools is that *the basis of relationships among teachers is the antithesis of the rationale of cooperative learning.* If by *professional* collegiality you mean an interest in and the existence of forums for serious discussion of a school's purpose, pedagogy, issues, and problems, very few schools are collegial, which is another way of saying that in the school culture (Sarason, 1996a) teachers do not and cannot learn from each other. Each teacher not only is and feels alone but over time the teacher *wants* to be left alone. To overcome that type of relationship is an uphill battle, as reformers have learned, and whatever success they have had has been limited, but that conclusion is based on the relatively few publications where that limited success has been described. We do not, of course, hear about the much larger number of instances where the reformers failed to achieve a meaningful collegial relationship among teachers, or where, when conditions changed, the small degree of success was no longer evident. I have known a number of these instances. In only one of these instances was I a frequent visitor–observer–consultant over a period of years and the reason for my interest in that effort was that the guiding rationale for the reform effort was highly similar to that which I have been discussing in these pages. The consequences have been, to say the least, encouraging, and to me it was and is inspiring. I urge the reader to read *The Courage to Change* by Paul Heckman (1995).

The preceding is by way of prologue to the question: How might a teacher–parent governing body be held accountable to external groups for its consistency between purpose, actions, and outcomes? That question presupposes that the governing body has been given the go ahead because: (1) It has committed itself to creating and sustaining contexts of productive learning; (2) It gives credible evidence that it has more than superficially worked through what that commitment will mean concretely and practically for everyone in the enterprise; and (3) It agrees to be observed, counseled, and judged by external groups, informally and formally. In brief, although the governing body is being given the opportunity to move in new ways in new directions consistent with an overarching purpose, it is made explicit that such a venture will be beset with predictable and unpredictable problems for which it should be encouraged and should feel obliged to seek advice, i.e., willingly to assume the stance that to be confronted with problems and to keep them "private" for fear of being seen as less than competent is other than a denial or misunderstanding of what a context of productive learning entails. *What the governing body seeks to create and sustain in the classroom is precisely the context it has to create and sustain for itself, and that will be unachievable as long as it isolates itself from ideas and suggestions of others, an isolation that can lead to anger, resentment, and the feeling of failure when at a later point formal, external judgment of the enterprise is made.* The board should never be in the position of the student who is puzzled and uncomprehending but fearful of asking questions, of appearing inadequate and dependent, of being seen as stupid. Have we learned nothing about unproductive learning?[1]

What I propose is that in any community three or four elementary schools be organized and governed by a parent–teacher governing body. Ideally there should be more than that but I assume that, initially at least, there will be relatively few schools where parents and teachers will take advantage of the opportunity to create and take responsibility for a new kind of school organization. If, however, the enabling legislation makes it possible, indeed encourages and supports regionalization, the number of schools could be more than a handful. In any event, each participating school would be a member of a council of these schools, on which each school is represented by a parent and a teacher. This council would have advisory, evaluative, and decision-making responsibilities. Let us begin with the advisory function.

By advisory function I mean that the council would be a forum where any and all issues, problems, and questions can be raised and discussed. It is a forum that makes it possible for its members to find out and discuss what others are doing, experiencing, and planning. That is to say, each member or school accepts the obligation to be forthcoming as a way of informing others and being informed by them. It is not a function intended to achieve uniformity in action and organization. There is uniformity only in the sense that every school has the overarching purpose of creating and sustaining contexts of productive learning, and there is awareness of and respect for the fact that there is no one right established way to realize that purpose. And there is uniformity of vision in that each school intends to be manifestly and dramatically different from the traditional conception of a school.

The forum is a means whereby its members can become available to each other. Availability can take diverse forms. A school can request that other members visit, observe, and discuss what it is doing, i.e., it seeks the opinions, reactions, and advice of others. Similarly, a member should feel free to request permission to observe another school because previous discussion suggested that it may have something to learn from what that school is doing. Availability can also mean *exchanging* resources on a temporary basis in ways that benefit both parties. Not all schools will have resources similar in kind or quality. I take that as a given as I also take as a given that when people share a common purpose, and relationships of respect and trust are forged because they are not in competition with each other and they need each other to gain public support, an exchange of resources (e.g., personnel, materials) that is mutually beneficial becomes a possibility, although the duration of the exchange may be temporary. And availability also makes possible a cooperative effort to identify and obtain resources that will be helpful to all. And precisely because this new kind of school will require public support the participating members, if only for purposes of survival, have to collaborate in a program of public education. *The name of the game is constituency building, constituencies that ultimately will decide the fate of these schools, and by constituency building I do not mean resort to self-serving propaganda but an openness of these schools to public scrutiny, i.e., to inform, to invite, to want to hear, to be able to listen.*

If schools can be faulted for anything, it is their almost total failure to educate the public about what is involved—philosophically, psychologically, and practically—in educating children who vary markedly on all factors conducive to learning. They ignored parents as well as the larger community for whom schools were strange, fortified, formidable enclaves under control of professionals whose implicit message to them was, "Send us your children, stay out of our way, we know what needs to be done, you will someday thank us." The social changes ushered in by World War II have exposed the self-defeating nature of that stance. We are used to hearing that war is too important to be left to the generals. Today, people are saying that education is too important to be left to the generals in education (That message is also being sent to the medical community; that is another but quite related story). I am in no way suggesting that the public has a folk wisdom others do not possess. I am not anti-professional. I have never argued that teaching is a simple affair that does not require a good deal of understanding not only about theory and knowledge but also what is involved in acting on that knowledge in ways productive for the learner. It is because preparatory programs so inadequately prepare teachers for what is an awesome and demanding task that I devoted a book to the issues (Sarason, 1992). Nor have I ever argued that those inadequacies and their baleful consequences were "willed" by anyone. There are no villains. But I have argued that in the case of schooling the political principle should be operative: If you are going to be affected by a policy or decision, you should stand in some relationship to the formulation of the policy and the making of a decision. That puts a special burden on teachers who, in accord with the principle, should be obliged to make their thinking, planning, and action understandable so that these stakeholders have a basis for forming their decisions. I reject the assumption that parents are unable and/or unwilling to be informed participants. But there is another, very practical reason for their participation: On their own educators cannot and will not be able to make whatever changes they seek to make, especially if those changes require altering the system. Without the involvement of parents and the larger community nothing will happen, except that the situation will predictably worsen. That explains why the council of schools I am proposing will be concerned as much with public education as it will be with the education of students.[2]

If I am describing a new relationship between parents and teachers, the reader should not overlook that *I am also describing a new relationship, not only among teachers in one school but also between teachers in one school with teachers in other schools sharing the same purposes and values.* The council is a mechanism for overcoming the growth-destroying consequences of the lonely teacher in an encapsulated classroom in an encapsulated school. The council would be a means for creating and sustaining contexts of productive learning for teachers and parents.

I have been discussing the advisory function of the council, its collegial aspects, its fostering of the acquisition of new knowledge on the basis of discussion of shared experience, of an expansion of the opportunity for direct observation of what others think and do, of a fostering of a sense of community, and of a more meaningful and deeper involvement in the communities in which these schools exist. Let us now turn to its evaluative functions.

The council will confront several questions. By what performance criteria should a participating school be judged? Who should make the judgment? When should the evaluation be made? What should happen in the case of a school receiving a negative judgment?

The first question can be put in another way: Since there is agreement that the primary purpose of schooling is to create and sustain contexts of productive learning, how will we know if the goal is, to a discernible extent, being realized or approximated? What and who will be sources of data?

1. Parents (other than those on the governing body) as well as others in the neighborhood and/or the community the school serves will be given an opportunity to express their views about the school. One way to do this, of course, is to have a general, open meeting where individuals can voice their opinions and observations. Another way is *randomly* to select a pool of parents, each of whom will be interviewed by the evaluating group. Neither of these ways is devoid of pluses and minuses. From the standpoint of getting candid and fleshed out reactions, I would prefer the individual interview but that preference, I admit, derives from my own experience. What an individual will say in a large public forum that individual may not say, or say as clearly or candidly, as in an individual interview where clarifying questions may be directed to the person. Regardless of method, the purpose is to obtain as clear an expression of opinion *and its basis* as possible, i.e., not to obtain "votes" for approval or disapproval. No one can say ahead of time which method will be the more productive of credible data. Whichever method or methods are used should not be viewed as locked in concrete as if they will not ever be in need of self-correction. One obvious safeguard is to experi-

ment with different methods in different schools. I use the word *experiment* advisedly to counter the present stance of governing bodies to require uniformity of procedure in their schools. A self-correcting system is one that provides a basis for when and how it should change its ways of operating. That basis cannot be provided by armchair reflection, or intuition, or the need to appear omniscient. The current system is the antithesis of a self-correcting one.

2. The evaluating group will have developed or will have been provided with, a schedule for observing students and teachers in the classroom. Are students actively interested and engaged in what they are doing both individually and in small working groups? Are they doing what they do only or largely as individuals in conformity with the instructions of the teacher? Are students encouraged and supported to work in small groups where they assume responsibility to address an issue or problem they and the teacher agree is important for their learning? Do the students appear free to ask questions, to seek guidance, to express opinions? Does it appear that there is a classroom "constitution" which is bidirectional in the sense that *both* teacher and student have rights and obligations which are clear, understandable, and willingly accepted? Is the teacher an instructor or an instructor *and* a coach, the only source of information and direction or an initiator of a process that does not subvert the initiatives of the students? Is student spontaneity seen as a distraction from or interference with a predetermined lesson plan, with the teacher's need for "order"? Is every child doing what every other child does? In brief, how different is the classroom context from what is now the modal American classroom context? I do not expect that the evaluating group or the council will have the time or expertise to develop an observational schedule that will lessen the distorting role of subjectivity. What I do expect and propose is that the enabling legislation for these schools provide funds for a research project to develop an observational schedule that will have acceptable reliability and validity. Let us not be detained here by who will do it, where it will be done, and how will it be done. The crucial point is that it will have to be done for the very practical reason that a self-improving and self-correcting system requires it, not for virtue in the abstract but for very practical-applied considerations.

Words like *experimenting* and *research* do not appear as line items in the budgets of school systems. They are viewed as frills, luxuries, or red flags to which an uncomprehending public will respond with angry rejection. I am suggesting a type of research that is targeted, applied, and necessary in a self-correcting system. To innovate deserves no badge of honor, as the history of educational research, as well as everyday experience, have documented *ad nauseam*. To innovate and to have even no semi-credible basis for deciding whether what you are doing is worth doing or continuing is fiscally, morally, and practically irresponsible. I am not suggesting that one sits still until observational and other procedures have been fully developed. But that in no way excuses you from taking seriously what you will need to do, and as quickly as possible, in order to be accountable to those you serve. Hope, prayer, and good intentions are frail reeds on which to depend as a basis for accountability.

3. For each student there will be a *chronological* record—call it a file, a portfolio, or whatever—of a student's work and any other relevant performance data. By record I mean samples of performance, not (only) numerical or alphabetical grades. By scrutinizing such a record, the evaluating team should be able rather quickly to determine whether the student is making no, little, or steady progress. In a separate meeting with the teacher, the team will seek explanation of why this or that child is showing little progress, and/or why the number of these children seems unacceptably or inexplicably large. Clearly, the teacher's explanation will be judged by or related to the classroom observations of the team. It may be that the teacher's explanation is not convincing, or it may be that the explanation might direct the team's attention to other features of the workings of that school. It should not be assumed that any negative finding is owing only to that teacher in that classroom, i.e., the school is an organization in which its parts are interconnected and what happens in one part may or may not reflect what is happening in other parts. It should be made explicit in diverse ways by the council that the evaluating team is not an adversary but it is an agent of the council, with the clear purpose of determining how well the school is consistent with its task of creating and sustaining contexts of productive learning for students *and* teachers. It is expecting too much to assume that the evaluation process will not engender some anxiety and defensiveness in the school's personnel. *However, I think that it is a difference that makes a difference if those doing the evaluating are themselves part of a school sharing the same purpose as the school being judged, i.e., the team is composed of their peers.* They are not administrative "superiors," that kind of school is not foreign to them, they have been or are still going through the same mill. Toward the end of a 2-day visit the team meets, decides on what will be the major points, and communicates them to the governing body and all of the other teachers. A report is then written and given to the council as well as to the school. No school will be evaluated before the last half of the second year of its existence. Before that, the school will have the council's advisory functions at its disposal. Depending on the substance of the report, the council may decide that no further evaluation need be done for 2 years; it may decide that an evaluation needs to be done in the following year. In either case, the initial evaluation will be an internal document, not one used for public consumption or education. Any school that undertakes to change, to organize itself differently, to think through

and implement the nature and consequences of a conception of productive learning—that is a school that will need advice, support, and time and should not be under the pressure of having to prove itself in less than 3 or 4 years. And by prove itself I do not mean the realization of all of its goals but rather that there is a reasonable basis for saying that it is on the right road. All subsequent evaluations would be public documents.

4. From each classroom in each school two students will be randomly selected for individual interviews. Here again the wording of questions, and the purpose of the interview to be communicated to the student, will have been developed and pretested to lessen the chances that the obtained answers are not being unwittingly slanted by the wording of the question. The purpose of the interview is to give the student an opportunity to express his or her opinions, likes, dislikes, and puzzlements about the school.

> You should not tell a student that the purpose of the interview is to find out how or if she likes school, a statement which, coming from an unfamiliar adult, may well convey to the child that he or she *should or is expected* to like school. One could say, "Adults are always asking other adults, such as parents and teachers, how they feel about this or that, whether they like this or that. But we don't ask those questions of students in regard to what they think and feel about what and how they are learning. So, we would be very grateful if you would help us understand how children think and feel about what they do in school. There are no right or wrong answers to our questions about how you think and feel about school. No one else will ever know what you tell us. And if you have any questions you want *us* to answer, just ask us and we will give you our answer.

The preceding is only by way of indicating two things. First, creating an atmosphere and framing questions are no cut and dried, mechanical affairs. Second, how students think and feel about their classroom and school is a crucial source of data relevant to the purpose of the school. What students think and feel should never be derogated or dismissed, at least by anyone who purports to understand and is committed to productive learning as the primary goal of schooling. If you do not think you *need* to know what children think and feel, you are not concerned with individuality or productive learning. You become a cause and overseer of unproductive learning. Knowing what students think and feel contributes to the self-correcting process.

5. What happens if the council decides that a school is blatantly inconsistent with its initial commitment to create and sustain contexts of productive learning? The substance and consequences of that decision will be largely determined by how the governing group of that school reacts to the decision. Can the council and that group agree on a remedial course of action? In the case where they cannot agree, the school will no longer be represented

on the council. It will go its own way. I am not in favor of dictating terms to a school the parents and teachers of which are in agreement about the direction they wish to go, however much I may disagree with their judgment and achievements.

Let me try to anticipate and confront the questions and criticisms of what I have thus far sketched because those questions and criticisms will arise again in response to proposals I will make in later pages. One reaction will be that my proposals are so beyond the realm of possibility as to warrant calling them sheer fantasy or utopian foolishness. That they are currently not in the realm of possibility I concede. But, I must remind the reader, I have written this book because I and many others in and beyond the field of education have concluded that it is beyond the realm of possibility to improve schools as long as reform efforts stay within and basically accept the current system, i.e., its governance, organization, and lack of priorities of purposes. The fact is that we are at a time, *as never before*, when increasing numbers of people are thoroughly disillusioned with the current system and fearful that its inadequacies will have increasingly negative effects on the social fabric. It is that observation and belief that should require us seriously to consider alternatives not as the stuff of fantasy but as a focus of attention and discussion in the marketplace of ideas and possibilities. The question the reader has to ask in the quiet of his or her nights is: Do I have reason to believe that the current system can be made to accomplish the goals we have set for it? And that question should lead to another question: How do I account for the past failure of reforms to have even minimally generalized desirable effects? Is the lesson we have learned that we need to do more of what we have done but we have to do it "better"? And what does "better" mean? Spending more money? Improving the quality of personnel? Raising standards? Making more creative use of technology? For example, consider the following, which a colleague sent to me:

- The National Education Summit will be hosted by Louis V. Gerstner, Chairman and CEO of IBM, and Wisconsin Governor Tommy G. Thompson, Chairman of both the National Governors' Association (NGA) and the Education Commission of the States (ECS).
- The goal of the Summit is to build commitment among participants for prompt actions that will help states and communities build consensus, develop and implement high academic standards, assessments and accountability.
- Participation at the Summit will be limited to 130 people, including all Governors, one key business leader from each state invited by the Governor, and a limited number of others, such as educa-

tors, state legislators, and chief state school officers. The Summit will also serve as a catalyst for other discussions and activities on standards, accountability, and technology.

- Two main issues will be addressed at the Summit: 1) how to develop and implement high academic standards for students, measure against such standards, and hold people accountable to those standards; and 2) how to infuse new technologies as tools for improving teaching and learning, and school improvement.

The colleague who sent this announcement to me has long been in the educational reform game, long enough to conclude that whatever his accomplishments they have been local, encapsulated, fragile, and too often of short duration. In his letter he says, "I've seen the agenda for Lou Gerstner's meeting. It is a total disaster. In fact, I'll include it here so you can see for yourself." It is a total disaster, the most recent in a long line of disasters too often preceded (as this one was) by publicity in the national media and conveying the message that there was nothing basically wrong with the existing system that raising standards and expectations and exploiting technology could not dramatically improve—as clear examples of wish-fulfilling fantasy as one will find. Mr. Gerstner's heart is in the right place; he is someone who wants to make a situation better than it is, but he has not the faintest knowledge of why the situation is as bad as it is, why it has been so intractable to past efforts. You would expect that the chairman and CEO of IBM would look at a problem in terms of the characteristics of the system in which the problem has arisen. It should be second nature to him and his advisors, but it is not. A couple of years ago when Mr. Gerstner took over IBM, it was in deep trouble. As I write, IBM has made a rather dramatic recovery. That recovery did not come about by changing the uses of technology within the organization. If and when the full story is written, I have no doubt that it will tell us how Mr. Gerstner confronted and drastically altered the system of a corporation that was failing. If anyone is indulging fantasy, it is people like Mr. Gerstner, and that includes many educators.

Another criticism by some readers is that I seem to be giving more and more authority to teachers and parents and in the process, asking them to give more time to participation in general and governance in particular. I cannot deny that there may be a kernel of truth to that criticism, but that is not a judgment anyone can make ahead of time. In a self-correcting system that kind of possibility will have to be confronted, but whatever changes will be required should in no way subvert the rationale for the purpose and governance of participating schools. I should point out that a participating school will be a *self-selected* school. That is to say, the teachers and parents of the school have chosen to take advantage of the opportunity and to assume the responsibility for that school and its relations to the council of similar schools.

Among psychotherapists there is a maxim: When a person decides on his or her own to seek help, that person has licked 50% of the problem. I regard that maxim as applicable to parents and teachers who seek to change their schools, their lives, and the quality of the school experience of their children. Especially in regard to teachers, reformers and administrators tell us time again how hard it is to overcome teacher resistance to change. What they overlook is the difference between teachers who *seek* to change and teachers who are *asked* to change for reasons of no intrinsic interest to and felt need by them. That is a difference that makes a very big difference for motivation, commitment, and personal sacrifice. It is the difference between a student who *wants* to be doing what he or she is doing and the student who does what he or she does because it is *required* by an adult who is insensitive to what the student thinks, feels, and wants to experience. Have we learned nothing of the difference in consequences between intrinsic and extrinsic sources of motivation in learning? Whatever I have proposed takes that difference very seriously because of its practical consequences. The modal American classroom contains few, if any, features of a context for productive learning. As I said earlier, you can find a classroom here and classroom there, an elementary school here and another one there, which have some, even many, of the ingredients of a context of productive learning. But those instances do not exist because the system encourages and supports them. *They exist despite the system, which explains why those instances do not and cannot generalize into the larger system.* It is an incompatibility that is lethal for generalization beyond the unusual instance. There are reformers who have demonstrated, heroically and with great expenditure of time, money, and energy, that contexts for productive learning can be created with remarkable results, but only in the classrooms that have been the reformers' focus and goal. Not only are these results often nonsustainable but to my knowledge no reformer has been able to demonstrate that the significance of these instances has in any way suffused the system. I do not accept the criticism that my proposals reflect my indulgence of the wish-fulfilling tendency. My rejoinder is that the criticism truly applies to those who believe that the rationale for and governance of the existing system can accomplish more than it does and can prevent a further deterioration, which I predict will be the case, despite the Mr. Gerstners of this world.

Another question that will have occurred to some readers: "You said earlier that in light of the additional time teachers will be giving to school affairs they should receive appropriate compensation. Does that mean that these teachers will be getting more than teachers in traditional schools? Will unions go along with that? Where will those additional funds come from?" Of course these teachers should receive more than teachers giving far less commitment and time to their schools. The additional compensation would be available to any teacher in any school that will be organized and governed as I have proposed. The additional compensation is not a merit increase but recognition of the fact that these teachers are giving far more of themselves than was the case in the past. Uniformity of pay is no justification for not rewarding a good deal of additional time beyond the usual school day, and it certainly should not act as a disincentive to taking on additional responsibilities. The additional funding would be authorized in the enabling legislation making these schools possible; that additional funding would not come from the local community.

There are other questions having to do with teacher tenure and evaluation, special services, and special education. Some of these questions I will take up in later chapters but, as I said earlier, I do not feel compelled, and I do not think it necessary, to take any or all of them up in detail. The reader may retort by saying that the devil is in the details, as it often is. I am not saying that these questions are mere details. What I am saying is that in the problem with which I am grappling the devil is less in the details (but still there) than in how clear one is about, and how seriously one takes, the need for a new system of governance whose overarching purpose is to create and sustain contexts for productive learning. The devil takes the form of permitting and sustaining us in the belief that the problem is in our schools, those physical structures called schools, and not in the system that we literally cannot see, we have to conceptualize it, and that when we try to comprehend we find disconnected parts, antagonistic parts, a bewildering diffusion of authority and accountability, a total lack of the self-correcting stance, an equally total incapacity to apply throughout the system that which has been learned from the few successes and the countless failures, and in no way is organized to create and sustain contexts of productive learning. What is devilish is how difficult it is for us to take our eyes off the school and ask: What is the system we are dealing with and on what philosophical, psychological, educational, political, and fiscal basis can we justify it? It took me years to take my eyes off the schools and ask that question. I had to answer that it was a system that, whatever its justification in earlier times, it was grievously inadequate in a society that had and is still undergoing social change. When I arrived at that conclusion, I saw that the time had arrived to begin to conceive of a system that stood a chance of providing schools the support and resources required to move in new directions with a clear purpose and with the responsibility to be accountable. You cannot change schools without changing the system that governs, constrains, and is a source of interference, not a source of support to, schools.

There is an omission in what I thus far have presented that readers, especially those who are educators, have undoubtedly noted. They have found themselves asking, "In all that you have proposed thus far about governance, you have never once mentioned the principal and his or her role. Was that deliberate and if so how can you justify it?" It was deliberate and I explain why in the next chapter.

NOTES

[1]Why is it that so many new settings fail of their purposes? My book, The Creation of Settings and the Future Societies (1972) deals with that question. Creating a new setting is a fascinating and difficult task; it is not an engineering, tooling-up task that, like the traditional concept of curriculum, assumes a step-by-step, time-driven process. No one creates a social–institutional setting literally to replicate a setting that already exists. The new setting is conceived as being in some way different from and superior to comparable settings. Settings fail of their purposes for many reasons, and one of the most frequent is forgetting or no longer taking seriously the way in which the setting was supposed to be different and better. Between purpose and action is a minefield of traps that takes attention away from the distinctive purpose, justifying the creation of the new setting.

[2]Edwin O'Connor's *The Last Hurrah* (1956) is the best book I have read about American politics. (The movie was terrible!). In a way for which the reader is unprepared, it is not until the final pages of the novel—when Skeffington is defeated for re-election— that we are given, and we understand, that his defeat reflected his insensitivity to the changes in the demography and attitudes of his constituency, i.e., the game and its scoring had changed but Skeffington had insulated himself from becoming aware of the changes. That lesson has yet to be learned by the educational community.

C H A P T E R   V I

Are Principals Necessary?

What *does* a principal do? What is a principal *supposed* to do? What would we *want* a principal to do? In each of these questions the reader should substitute the verb *be* for the verb *do* as a way of indicating that as important as what a principal does is how that person is regarded and judged by others, and that cannot be determined by listing or describing what he or she does. How we see ourselves in a particular role, how we want others to see us in that role, may or may not be discrepant with how others see us. I may see myself as a friendly, cooperative neighbor always available for requests for my presence, advice, chitchat, and the like. My neighbors may or may not see me that way! I did not sit down with them to get agreement about what we can or should expect of each other and how we should resolve differences of opinions, frequency of interaction, and obligations of each to the other. Our relationship is not governed by a "constitution" or any explicit rules and regulations. There is an unexpressed assumption that each knows what neighborliness and courtesy entails, an assumption that may be proved right or wrong. If we are proved right, we are pleased and it may even be that the basis of the relationship widens and deepens in ways that alters the regularities of our social existence. If we are proved wrong, so be it, our social existence is not likely to be much affected. There are those instances, of course, where neighborliness becomes a deep friendship, there is a falling out, interactions cease or become chilly, or very infrequent, i.e., neither of us is in doubt that we are in agreement to stay out of each other's way, the communication or message is indisputably nonverbal and very clear.

Teachers and the principal are not neighbors. Each has a role established not only by tradition but by a written job description defining the purpose, functions, scope, and obligation of the role. The job description usually will not be an all-encompassing one because of the "of course" stance that everyone knows his or her role so that not everything needs to be spelled out. For example, one of the things that does not get spelled out is what the purposes of the school are and that each role in its own distinctive way furthers those purposes. That assumption is far more often than not valid. What purposes are and how they are prioritized, and how purposes are to be realized are not spelled out, i.e., it is expected that, whatever the role, the person is prepared to bring that realization about, a result that will be measured by age-graded tests specified by the system. The teacher teaches; he or she has some latitude in deciding the pedagogy that will be employed in the classroom. The principal supervises: He or she has "super" vision and knowledge required to direct and organize the school to meet its purpose. The teacher is a "part," not one who sees the whole picture. The principal knows all of the parts that he or she is expected to interconnect and organize in support of the school's purposes.

So, let us ask, what do teachers say that a principal does? I have been querying teachers about this for over 40 years, which is why when I wrote the first edition of *The Culture of the School and the Problem of Change*, I briefly and ever so gently indicated that it was not all that clear to me why a school needed a principal. Here are the most frequent replies.[1]

1. The principal is the only formal conduit for information, directives, rules, and regulations from the school district's administrative, policy-making hierarchy.
2. The principal handles all sorts of emergencies, e.g., a teacher or student becomes ill; substitutes need to be obtained; police need to be contacted; notifying authorities when the heating or electrical system is dysfunctional or the roof is leaking, etc.
3. The principal has scheduling responsibilities, such as for buses and field trips.
4. It is the principal who determines student transfer, equity in class size, investigates unusual absences, and manages issues surrounding expulsion and suspension, and complaints by and conflicts with parents.
5. The principal is the intermediary between the teacher and a variety of district-wide supervisors and special personnel, especially in regard to students who may be eligible for or require special education and services.

6. The principal carries out procedures for and makes decisions about the evaluation of teachers.
7. The principal is the one to whom a teacher can bring personal and professional issues affecting that teacher's needs and performance.
8. The principal's office is where important records are kept for each student that are available to and necessary for teachers and diverse supervisors.

It was inconceivable to teachers that a school did not need someone in the formal role of principal, someone whose responsibility it was to take care of myriads of details, maximizing the chances that a teacher could teach and students could learn in an efficient and effective manner. Only very rarely did a teacher describe the principal as one who is an instructional leader, a source of new ideas and practices, a convener of forums where professional issues in that school and/or in the field at large were discussed and evaluated. *It was hard to avoid the conclusion that for teachers that principal was best who did not intrude into the domain of teachers: the classroom. That is precisely how teachers viewed each other, i.e., a teacher did not want or like any other teacher who by action or words passed judgment on his or her style of teaching or classroom management or student achievement. And that was, of course, true for how principal and teacher regarded parents.*

How does the principal see him- or herself and how does he or she see teachers (in which role the principal once was)? The self-perception of the principal is that of a person who has a plethora of duties and responsibilities to all those in the school as well as to those administratively above the principal—all of which requires time, patience, fortitude, and a high level of sensitive diplomacy. The principal sees the role as "in between" the needs and problems of students and teachers, on the one hand, and policies, pressures, and attitudes of those in higher positions, on the other hand. What the principal wants to do is often in conflict with what he or she can or is allowed to do. As one principal put it, "This job prepares you to be a tightrope walker in the circus, except that as a principal I don't feel I have a safety net." The principal sees teachers as varying dramatically in interpersonal style, in their classroom behavior, in their understanding of students, in the psychology undergirding their pedagogical practices and goals, in their openness to new ideas and change, certainly in the frequency with which they bring him or her small or large problems, and in their willingness to go "beyond the call" to make the school a better one. The principal would like to be—as he or she once expected to be—an educational–instructional leader but that expectation foundered on teachers' resistance to and resentment of the principal's efforts to be other than an infrequent visitor to the classroom for the purposes of giving advice and evaluation.

In previous publications I have attempted to describe and explain what teachers and principals have told me and why it should occasion no surprise that *professional* attitudes and relationships are what they are. What I wish to point out here are several features noteworthy for their absence. To understand a school we pay attention to its behavioral and programmatic regularities, and to public and private expressions of feeling and attitude, and other features that can be scaled on the explicit–implicit continuum. That kind of approach can be informative and instructive, especially in instances where the school is an untroubled one by whatever criteria you are employing. That is to say, for all practical purposes the school is regarded as doing its job well. I may strongly disagree, but I have to admit that everyone in and around that school is satisfied with what it accomplishes. There are few such schools. There are a great many schools that are troubled. Indeed, in the post–World War II era there has been a steady, escalating dissatisfaction with schools as well as of the number of people—outside as well as inside the schools—who find themselves judging schools as lost causes. In regard to these schools, paying attention to their implicit–explicit regularities and dynamics will be limited in remedial or preventive significance. What is required is that we ask: What is absent in these schools? What is not there that should be there? Why do these absences go unnoticed and undiscussed? Is it that they once were considered but rejected for what were then considered good and sufficient reasons?

For example, there is no agreement among school personnel about the overarching purpose of schooling. That may sound ridiculous and strange because it is self-evident that school personnel seek to help students to acquire knowledge and skill; to be motivated to learn, to acquire a sense of moral and civic responsibility, and more. What is obvious is that they claim a number of purposes that are more or less coequal in importance. But what is the pedagogical–psychological rationale that determines how any of these goals can be achieved? To that question there is very little agreement on the level of words and action. The relation of rationale to actual practice is ambiguous in the extreme. What is absent, now and in the past, is a discussion of alternative rationales and their significances for practice, a discussion without which each teacher justifies going his or her own way oblivious to, disinterested in, and with no feeling of responsibility for what other teachers do. There is an assumption that the school is a professional community the members of which assume the obligation as a group to analyze and discuss pedagogical–psychological issues, controversies, and new ideas that arise in the field of education, and to do this not only to broaden their knowledge but to determine whether and/or how that knowledge applies or should apply to their school. *Not only is that tradition and that kind of forum absent in the school, it is not even required, supported, or encouraged by the system, or initiated and sus-*

tained by the principal who is quite aware of the limits both of his or her power and influence. There is no professional collegiality or community, no agreed-on means or procedures for change and self-correction, no educational leadership. The school contains individualists whose individuality is in an institutional context where it cannot be scrutinized, influenced, or capitalized on by others. Teachers cannot learn from other teachers or from the principal. The governance system socializes them to accept and conform to a predetermined, calendar-driven routine, however much that may conflict with what they think should be, i.e., with their individuality. And it is not much different in the case of the principal who over time gives up the fantasy of being a leader and reluctantly resigns him- or herself to being a manager. No one is or feels accountable for the school as a whole when any of its diverse purposes are not being achieved. If anyone, it is the principal who is held responsible because he or she is expected to be on top of things, to identify problems and take corrective action, an expectation the principal resents because it assumes he or she can "fix it," legislate change, and the problem is solved. There are instances, to be sure, where the principal deserves criticism, and sometimes termination, but that raises this question: How come the system did not know (or if it knew but did nothing) that these principals were inadequate until trouble could not be ignored? The existing system is based on an orientation of repair, not on one of prevention. *And it is the preventive orientation that is almost totally absent in the existing governance. A system that devotes a significant portion of its resources to repair is on a treadmill that will never stop, and it will have to increase that portion, as has been blatantly clear in the post–World War II era.*[2]

Why did I say nothing about a principal in the proposal I sketched in the previous chapter? I must remind the reader that the starting point was a school where parents and teachers had reached agreement that their school would be one that would take a particular psychological–pedagogical rationale seriously and that meant they would judge school-classroom organization, the role of the teacher, the relationships among teachers, the coequal status of parents and teacher, time perspective, and all other related variables by how consistent and well action reflects that rationale. And I connected each school to a council of similar schools as a way of introducing a self-correcting stance and procedures. But all of this requires that those who govern the school are willingly part of a group in frequent contact with each other, observers of each other, in explicit agreement not only about an overarching purpose but also about their obligation to insure that the group has the features of a family and avoids the alienating consequences of an individualism that puts the "me" above and before all others. Individuality is both to be respected and treasured and its expressions need not be in conflict with group pressure to conform. The time to worry is when individuality is inhibited and the group presents a facade of agreement that is not only superficial but is intended to mask the stresses and strains of individuality. In how many faculty meetings do teachers feel safe and free to express differences of opinions, to put out on the table their ideas, concerns, and criticisms? To how many of the once-a-month faculty meetings do teachers go with eager anticipation that they will be thinking and deciding about ideas, issues, and plans that are of significance to all?

I did not decide ahead of time that there would be no principal. I did start with the conviction that whatever scheme I devised demanded that all participants shared the same responsibilities, obligations, and accountability. It was *their* school, *their* creation, *their* professional obligation to sustain. They agreed to be masters of their fate and captains of their souls, in line with what a poet once said. That soon forced on me the recognition that the traditional basis for the role of principal not only gave that person more power than anyone else but, no less important, the daily activities of the principal remove him or her from the classroom, one of the crucial places where the relation between rationale and purpose becomes manifest in practice. In the existing system the principal is an agent of an administrative superior who is even more removed from the classroom, a place he or she once knew but has long since forgotten. Finally, the empirical evidence is that principals are managers, not educational leaders; by virtue of who selects, appoints, and evaluates them the principal has a dual allegiance: the school and the system. In practice, the principal is as much, and often less, accountable to the one as to the other, which is why as time goes on the idealistic principal slowly but steadily becomes a more or less passive cog in the system.

Who, then, would do all of the managerial duties of the principal? I refrain from going into detail about alternative ways the school's governing body might consider. For example, in a previous chapter I said that a critic could rightfully argue that my proposal places somewhat awesome responsibilities on school personnel that would require a great deal of time. Now, he would say, I am compounding the felony of unrealistic expectations by saying that they could somehow or other mange to cover for whatever principals now do. I can assure the critic that I am aware of expecting a lot, but I do not expect that those expectations can be met only by heightened motivation, self-sacrifice bordering on masochism, and the lure of an increased income. What I propose is that the school be able to add two teachers to their faculty, and for several reasons. Because that school will be taking the implications of productive learning seriously, it will not be possible, and would not be desirable, to stay within the one classroom–one teacher mold. To what extent those kinds of instances occur will be determined by the decisions and planning of the governing body. There is no one, and only one, way of going from rationale to how classrooms are organized and interrelated. On the level of appearance I do not expect that these schools will look like clones, as is the case now. The second reason is that the additional teachers will make it possible for the faculty to figure out how to do those tasks the principal now does. The reader should keep in mind that some of the things a principal must now do because the system requires it may not be required by the governing group. The school is not part of a system that by its nature fosters a uniformity among schools by a detailed set of rules, regulations, and directives that constrain, constrict, and direct. A school's individuality will be determined by the parents and teachers and not by "higher ups" who are far more concerned with uniformity than with individuality. And, I must remind the reader, I am not proposing that schools be given license to do anything they want to but rather that they have the freedom to work out what needs to be worked out consistent with the overarching purpose to which they are committed and for which they will be accountable.

My proposals are, obviously, not intended as a manual. Manuals are justified if, and only if, the point has been reached where one is describing a process for which there is evidence, not only opinion, that it accomplishes its stated purpose. Before you write a manual intended to be helpful, it should have been preceded by at least three discrete steps. The first step is conceiving what the relationship might or should be between purpose and the process to realize that purpose, never forgetting that your initial conception is just that: an approximation. The second step is to implement that conception with the clear expectation that you will have to change the process in some ways, and that change will derive from self-correcting procedures to protect you against seeing only what you want to see. To have no built in self-correcting procedures is irresponsible. The next step occurs when you are satisfied that you can justify a manual that lays out the process in clear detail, noting issues and questions alerting the reader to the fact that the manual is a guide that does not absolve the reader of responsibility to exercise judgment in its use. There are or should be *post-manual* steps that lead to improvements in light of what users have experienced and reported. What I am describing is a process of continual improvement having all of the features operative in the development of a material product, object, and mechanism. It is a process whereby the Wright brothers' achievements led to the modern jet airplane, and how the earliest computers led to those we now have. Powering that process was the need and commitment on the part of developers to confront defects and inadequacies, to seek and make improvements that will not only serve the purposes of interested "customers" but by those improvements will enlarge the size of the customer pool. The self-correcting, developmental process has been extraordinarily clearly described by Kenneth Wilson and B. Daviss (1996) in their seminal book *Redesigning Education*. They do not leave you in doubt that our existing educational system is one that totally lacks features of a self-correcting system.

Some readers will ask: How applicable is a self-correcting, developmental process for inanimate objects to human systems? The fact is that it was long applicable. On February 16, 1996, the PBS television station in New York (Channel 13) devoted a program to the films of Stanley Donen, who either conceived and/or directed some of the best movie musicals of the past half century. The program was not designed to illustrate the self-correcting, developmental process. Nevertheless, Mr. Donen described in gripping detail what is involved, what can take place, what is predictable and unpredictable when one goes from an initial idea or vision to a finished product. A film director, of course, is in and directs a system containing an assortment of people. What Mr. Donen describes is how at each point in the making of his films he judges how well a particular scene is consistent with his initial conception of that scene. That is why a scene, a "take," may be done over and over again. It is indeed rare that a scene will require only one take. *The point is that at every step in the process the director (as well as many others who are part of the process) is or should be obliged to pass judgment on the consistency between initial purpose or conception and its visual representation on film.* At the end of a day of shooting the director and others not only look at the rushes for that day but they do so from a self-critical stance. Mr. Donen gives some instructive and amusing examples of how solutions to problems unpredictably occur. So what happens when the film is presumably finished? It is previewed by small audiences considered representative of the much larger audiences they want to come to pay to see the film. How did they respond? What did they like or dislike? What changes do we have to make? Long before politicians "discovered" and began to use focus groups, Hollywood had already been using them. Changes fall into two categories: those that will reflect initial purpose or conception better, and those that, because of diverse pressures from diverse sources, are not in the spirit of the initial purpose. Here again Mr. Donen gives us examples of why changes in initial purpose and conception should not be lightly accepted. In any event, the self-correcting stances does not guarantee that the sought-for goals will be reached. However, the absence of the self-correcting process guarantees that you will learn nothing from experience, a judgment amply justified by the reform efforts that start with "Model A," implement it, and never get to a "Model B" into which the lessons learned about the inadequacies of "Model A" have been incorporated. You start and persist with "Model A," and you end with it. That is a recipe for standing still.

Let us return to the principal. I have known or read about principals, albeit very few in number, who were absolutely crucial for the degree to which and the ways in which they were able to bring about changes *approximating* what I have envisioned in my proposals. Here are some instructive features.

1. The school was hurting, i.e., teachers, parents, and the surrounding community were very dissatisfied with what the school was and accomplished. No one needed to be convinced that changes were in order.
2. In most cases a new principal was brought on the scene with the message, "Do something, do anything, but clean up the mess." Implicit in the message was, "We will support you. We will stay out of your way."
3. These principals came to see that dramatic changes were necessary in teacher–student, teacher–teacher, teacher–parent, school–community relationships. These principals seemed to act as if the principal and all others relevant to the school could indeed organize themselves differently and move in new directions if there they shared a common purpose.
4. No one was in doubt that spearheading these changes and altering attitudes and relationship with consequences no one had ever had grounds to think possible was an assertive, supporting, "street smart," charismatic principal who rarely was in his or her office but all over the school and its community surround. Also, that principal under stood well that in the "old" school students were bored, unmotivated, and passive. The purpose of schooling and the obligations of those responsible for the school were to change the students' relation to and perception of learning.
5. Not the least of the principal's purpose and achievements was locating and obtaining *human* resources in the community that had never been obtained before. The walls between the school and its community surround became very porous.
6. There were times when the school had opposition from the system because the school clearly went beyond existing rules and regulations. The constituencies related to and supportive of the school were bulwarks allowing the principal to avoid submitting to the pressures for uniformity.

I have also observed other instances where schools were hurting, actions were required, and a new principal was installed. The most that can be said about these instances is that things got quieter, where necessary "law and order" established, but virtually nothing else changed. The major difference, and I would say the sole one, between these principals and the much smaller group I discussed previously, was that the latter, far more than the former, understood

that if you wanted to change classrooms you had to change the basis of relationships in the classroom, in the school, between schools and parents. Those
principals were not managers, they were leaders in contexts that included and
extended beyond the school. I have no basis whatsoever for criticizing them
or downplaying their accomplishments. These are instances where I thank God
for big favors. But— there is always a but—what conclusions are we justified
in drawing about their significance for changing contexts of *unproductive* learning in American schools that are not hurting, even though teachers and students are mired in traditions and routines that are antithetical to productive
learning for both groups?

Some readers will ask, "Are you not pulling the rug out from under
your proposals? If there are instances where principals have made a big difference by creating the kind of school context you consider so important,
would it not be less complicating, more realistic, and much less radical to come
up with proposals to increase the quantity and quality of principals?" I have
to ask those readers whether they are conceding the point that an overwhelming number of principals are not now possessed of the rationale and
vision to do justice to the spirit and substance of my proposals?

I am aware that in recent years there have appeared new programs for
educators, primarily administrators, on leadership. I have been acquainted with
several of them and their developers are quite explicit when they say that
these programs represent a departure from past programs that turned out
managers, not leaders. The emphasis in these new programs is on organizational theory, group relations, and the research literature on school and system reform. In none of these programs, however, is there critical
reexamination either about the form and features of the existing system or
the purposes of schooling or how the two are at cross purposes or how the
former places extraordinary constraints on the latter. These are programs
that in no way challenge the existing system or even the organization of a
school. They accept the form of what now exists and seek to enable the educator to make it work better. They do not seek to *re*form the system but to
reenergize it, to handle more smoothly and creatively the stresses and strains,
the conflicts, the sore points that now characterize it. They are essentially
preparing their students to work within the system. Needless to say, without
in any way suggesting that these programs are without any merit, I regard
them as Band-Aids, as forms of holding actions that, I predict, time will expose
as well-meaning failures, complete failures. As long as they remain within
the confines of the existing system, that system will extinguish whatever motivation or fantasies the students of these programs may have had about contexts of productive learning. Now let me state a fact, not an opinion, about
that very small group of principals I described earlier: They did what they
did *despite* the system and their formal training, not *because* of them. They

were driven by bitter experience to adopt a point of view and courses of action they had not heretofore contemplated. They are the exceptions. They are not the rule. There are always exceptions. In this case they are exceptions that should not lull one into believing that programs in educational administration or leadership are or can be an answer. They are part of the problem, not of the solution.

The exceptional schools I described are incomprehensible without the presence of an exceptional person. That is a glimpse of the obvious, but it is no less obvious that when that person departs, the scene can change in untoward ways. That need not happen, but it very frequently does happen, especially because the school is embedded in a system that regards it as an anomaly in a sea of uniformity. It is not unusual for the system to select a principal who is less of a sore thumb than the departing principal. Question: *Why is it that in these exceptional cases the existing system over time did not seek to encourage and spread some of the achievements of these exceptional people and their accomplishments?* The general answer is that the existing system is not one that learns. It is an unproductive learning system or, put in another way, it does little or nothing to change a situation unless a crisis or catastrophe erupts and cannot be ignored. In any event, I consider it a very mixed blessing for a non-traditional school to depend on an exceptional principal for its continuation. My proposal, requiring as it does a semi-autonomous governing body committed to a particular rationale, is far more likely to preserve that rationale when a member of the governing body departs. There are no guarantees, of course, but I do expect that precisely because the parents and teachers of a school have agreed to take the responsibility to move in a new direction that they will select new faculty who will carry on the spirit of the rationale. And I also expect that among the teachers and parents more than one type of leader will emerge. When we think of leaders we ordinarily think of one person who is "above" others, a person who has been granted or who has assumed formal power or authority; all others are followers. I do not think my experience is atypical when I say that in any school I have known well—and that includes many ghetto schools—there were always several teachers with the potential to exercise leadership in different aspects of the educational enterprise, and I am not referring to a desire for power. I am not one who overevaluates teachers. Talents, gifts, and capacities are distributed among them no differently than among those in any other professional group, and that is true for personality characteristics as well. What I am saying is that in the present system, the characteristics of many teachers are neither recognized nor exploited. The socialization process effectively dilutes or even extinguishes those characteristics. We are used to hearing that the purpose of schooling is for "each child to develop his or her potential to the fullest extent." Under the best of circumstances we will fall short of the mark, and under present circumstances we fall short of the mark to an unconscionable degree, and one reason is that to a similar degree the potentialities of teachers cannot be realized in the present system. What we want for students we *have* to want for teachers of those students. As I have said countless times, teachers cannot create and sustain contexts of productive learning for students if those contexts do not exist for teachers. It is no wonder that so many teachers wither on the vine, just as it is no wonder that the bulk of students view learning as a process to meet the demands of teachers and not one that reflects their individuality.

I know that the omission of the principal in my proposal will get short shrift in many quarters. That omission is in no way a reflection of my regard for the motivations, hopes, and capacities of principals. Indeed, it is my opinion that on average those who became principals in the last two decades are far more sensitive to and knowledgeable about the inadequacies of the system than in previous decades. But they are in a system they know needs to be changed, and they cannot participate in that change. In my book, *The Case for Change. Rethinking the Preparation of Educators* (1992), I expressed the view that the lack of *any* overlap between the preparation of teachers and administrators maximized rather than minimized their understanding of and working with each other. My criticism of the preparation of both groups assumed that if these programs were appropriately changed, the educational system would improve. I soon came to see that that assumption was not warranted. As long as the system remains what it is, it will subvert any improvements these programs would initiate.

I propose that colleges and universities have a *single* program for *educators,* not one for teachers, one for administrators, and one for leaders. Obviously I would want that program to take seriously the substance, spirit, and implications of my proposal so that those who traverse that program will be able and will be expected to be in more than one role in a school. That will be a far more comprehensive, demanding, and prolonged program than now exists and would, for the first time, prepare its students to take on one of the most essential characteristics of a professional: to determine the conditions in which he or she will render services to others and, to put it negatively, to refuse to do what others require them to do because it is a violation of what they believe to be in the interests of those with whom they work and whom they serve. In the existing system educators are not professionals, they are hired hands doing the bidding of others, conforming to a system most of them know to be inadequate at best and bankrupt at worst.

I shall have more to say about preparatory programs in a later chapter. I brought it up here in part to emphasize that colleges and universities are part of the system and to talk about school reform or systemic reform without talking about reform of preparatory programs is to reveal a most superficial conception of system. Colleges and universities do not "govern" schools, but they mightily determine what happens or does not happen in schools. To leave them out of the picture, to look to them as sources of answers to our present educational ills sets the stage for disillusionment. What I am saying here has been said privately to me by more than a handful of faculty in our colleges of education. In their own ways they valiantly seek to change the colleges of education in which they are members. But they know that, like a school system, these colleges have many unconnected parts, conflicts about turf, and virtually no agreement about the purposes of schooling and how to achieve those purposes. Learning from and with each other in colleges of education is as infrequent as it is among parts and individuals in the public schools!

NOTES

[1]The first edition was published in 1971, the second in 1982 when I added chapters on special education. In 1996 the book was republished with the title, *Revisiting the Culture of the School and the Problem of Change,* the word *revisiting* signifying my answer to the question: In what ways and to what extent has the culture of the school changed in the quarter of a century since the book was first published? That question required a good deal of thinking and many additional pages. It was in the course of thinking and writing that I decided that I had to write this book on governance, albeit I had resisted doing that because it was a problem that was best approached by a group of people who, however they differed on a host of factors, were in agreement that a new governance system was needed.

[2]In a most recent book, Cowen et al. (1996) describes the history, rationale, implementation, and outcomes of the longest, most carefully researched, preventive oriented program in American education. You would think that in light of what he and his colleagues have demonstrated over four decades that the stakeholders in the governance system of our schools would have sought to adopt his program. Today that program is in place in 700 schools, here and abroad. Given the thousands of schools in this country, would you not expect that it would have become (deservedly) more widespread? I continue to be both amazed and disheartened by how many people in the educational arena are unaware of what he has accomplished. Forums where new ideas and worthy programs are read and discussed are absent in schools.

Redefining Resources

The substance of this chapter concerns issues only hinted at in relation to the elementary school, although these issues are crucial for every school. If these issues are crucial, they have been relatively unexamined; more correctly, they have not been reexamined. The issues are implied in several questions. How do we define a resource? How might we redefine a resource? How does tradition prevent us from even examining how we might redefine a resource? It was clear in the previous chapter that I was redefining the roles of teachers and parents. The redefinition was based on a rejection of the tendency to use labels as indicating the resources people possess. So, for example, it used to be that the label or category *woman* meant a person who could sew, cook, clean, manage a household, and play a major role in rearing children. If she was unmarried, she might become a teacher where her "maternal" qualities were appropriate to educating the young. If she wanted to write novels or poetry, she was well advised to keep what she wrote private or seek to publish it with a masculine name. Being perceived as wanting to do what men do was a source of criticism and derision. Women in the armed forces? Women as pilots of military aircraft or members of a crew exploring space? Women as heads of large corporations? Those who in earlier days saw women in these roles would have been considered more than foolish. A woman was a woman, period. A label tells us a lot of things, not the least of which is what an individual does and what that individual should not be expected to do or could do. Labels restrict as well as describe the resources an individual possesses. We, of course, know after a moment of reflection that the individual does many things not referred to by the label, but when the label refers to a working role, these other things are of little interest to those with whom that person works.

There is one time in the life of a society when the conventional use of labels undergoes change, and that is when it is catapulted into a major war, e.g., World War II. Personnel shortages, both within and outside the military, did not permit, for purposes of matching person to job, a rigid adherence to conventional job labels and descriptions. One had to go beyond labels to an examination of an individual's life experiences and interests to do the matching. As a result, during the World War II years a large number of people were assigned to tasks they had never contemplated but that, they discovered, altered dramatically their perception of their capabilities and their career plans after the war was over. I have no doubt that there were mismatches, but there is no evidence whatsoever that, in general, individuals did not adapt competently to new roles and responsibilities. When the war was over the society tended to revert (for a time) to its accustomed stance of judging the resources of individuals by narrowly defined, conventional labels.

Let me give two examples more directly relevant to my present purposes.

A colleague, Richard Sussman, visited a professor he had had in child development in Teachers College, Columbia University. He met with her and her graduate assistants to find out what research they were planning and carrying out in regard to schools. They outlined a series of researches they wished to do with elementary school children, research that would require several schools. However, they said, they had been unsuccessful in getting permission from schools to carry out the studies. At one point Sussman asked: "If I could make available to you a dozen highly selected high school seniors, would you and your assistants be willing to explain your study to them and train them to collect your data? [Asking that question reflected the fact that a high school with which he was associated had a "'problem' keeping bright, college-bound seniors from goofing off in their final semester. Dr. Sussman's assets were his knowledge that he could make elementary schools available.] Also, would you be willing to give them a mini-course in organizing and analyzing data?" Needless to say, Sussman had determined that the high school students were adequate to the tasks. Also, again needless to say, the professor and her assistants did not look kindly at his offer. Use high school students to collect data? Teach them to organize and analyze data? Their reservations were dispelled when he played his trump card: "If you are willing to use these students, I am quite sure I can make available to you as many elementary schools as you need." The project went so well that at its completion the students were invited to give a colloquium at Teachers College and later made a presentation to their board of education. Money was never in the picture.

To the college professor, high school students were high school students, period. That is not unusual because when we say that someone is a student, whether in the first grade or in high school, we tend to be more impressed with what he or she does not know and cannot do than with what he or she does know and is interested in. It is only slightly unfair to say that our stereotype of student emphasizes deficits and not assets. But it is not unfair to say that our tendency to categorize people—to attribute to them all the characteristics of the abstract category—gets in our way of redefining them, of seeing them as multifaceted individuals.

One more example. This concerned a plan I devised whereby Yale University faculty and graduate students would set up, without cost, a department of psychology in a high school. And by department I meant one that spanned the traditional areas in that field.

Several school systems were quite eager for us to use their high schools. Although we monotonously repeated that there was a fair chance that we would fall on our faces, that we did not view ourselves as experts in high school teaching, that graduate and even (highly selected) undergraduates would be involved in addition to faculty, that we did not want to be viewed as in any way impinging on any one else's territory—the response was uniformly enthusiastic and for two reasons. First, in each school system there were some personnel who asserted that I was a responsible individual who knew something about schools. Second, they said they had so many unmotivated students, and since psychology was intrinsically fascinating to everybody (they obviously never sampled undergraduate opinion!), they could only see our involvement as helpful. In essence, we had no "port of entry problem" to speak of. The fact that we posed no credentialing issues was also a plus. The project lasted one year and could not be continued because of a variety of serious illnesses in my family that made planning and commitment an exercise in futility. The school was eager for us to continue. Not only was the teaching perceived as successful, but in diverse ways our group became involved with different individuals, groups, and departments in ways that we had hoped for and that were regarded by school personnel as extremely helpful in achieving desired changes.

And now for the major point: We came to the schools. We offered certain services and a long range plan which the schools saw as a possible help to a serious problem. It never occurred to them to come to us. Given their accustomed way of viewing the community, it could not occur to them that perhaps they had a "right" to request and even to demand help. They viewed the problems with which they were faced as their responsibility, solvable either by existing resources or additional ones they could buy (knowing full well that they would never be able to buy resources adequate to their needs as they defined them). They cannot take the stance that one of their major tasks is to refuse to assume exclusive responsibility for or to be seen as having the expertise to deal adequately with all the problems existing in schools. They cannot say aloud what they say privately: We will never have financial resources to cope effectively with our problems; unless we have call on community resources—unless we make the community share responsibility—the disparity between what we can do and what needs to be done will continue, and perhaps become greater.

What deserves emphasis in this example is that it could never occur to school people that there could be people in the community whose professional self-interests might lead them to provide services to schools on a quid pro quo basis: "If you do this for us, we will do that for you." No one has to tell educators that they have problems for which they need help. And no one needs to tell educators that there are people in the community who can be of help to them with those problems. But it is almost axiomatic in the stance of educators that these community people cannot be approached without the carrot of compensation. "They are busy people. They probably do not have enough time in a day to do all they want and need to do. How can we ask them to give us time free for nothing?"—that is the usual view of educators of the availability of community resources. It is, obviously, a realistic view but only if your approach is: "We have a problem. You can be of help to us. Are you willing to give us that help for which we cannot pay?" In other words, you appeal to their altruism, not to their self-interests, i.e., to the possibility that providing the help will in some way have a significant payoff for them.

I have no objection to appealing to people's altruism. Indeed, as I stated in the example, educators have a "right" to request and even demand that community people and agencies give of their time and skills to schools, i.e., they have an obligation to do so. But as long as educators see themselves, and therefore are seen by others, as solely responsible for what happens in schools—a stance that keeps private inadequacies that should be made public—they tend neither to request nor demand. Instead, they devote their energies internally to get increases in school budgets that would permit them either to add personnel or to pay for externally situated resources. When, as is usually the case, those increases are not forthcoming, educators feel rejected and derogated and resign themselves to making do with what internal resources they possess. Their feeling of rejection when the political system fails to give them what they perceive they need is precisely the feeling they expect to have if they approached community individuals and agencies hat-in-hand, that is, as beggars. Educators have never been able to say out loud, "We have never had, will not have, and perhaps should not have, sufficient resources internally to accomplish our tasks the way we want and the public expects. Unless and until we have call on community resources we will be unable to compensate *to any extent* for the brute fact of limited resources."

If I have no objections to appealing to people's altruism, neither do I expect such appeals to be very fruitful. It is not that I think people generally are without altruistic feelings but rather that the appeal to self-interest (which is not to be confused with selfishness) is far more likely to be fruitful. If that is true, as my experience clearly suggests, the task of the educator is to be as knowledgeable as possible about the self-interests of community individuals and agencies so as to be able to determine when the self-interests of educators and others can result in an exchange of resources.

No money, no resources. When educators begin to see that this is not as true as it needs to be or should be, that what they have may be seen by others (in terms of their self-interests) as assets, that bartering for and exchanging resources can engender and sustain satisfying and productive relationships, that the failure to accept the fact that resources are always limited constrains creativity in thinking and acting—in short, when educators can begin to alter their way of defining resources, the concept of community participation will become more than what it now is: empty, unproductive rhetoric.

On any one day hundreds (perhaps thousands) of academics are carrying out research in schools. Their expectation is that schools have an *obligation* to permit research because the findings will add to the cumulative knowledge about how to improve schooling. I italicize obligation to emphasize that the appeal is to the altruism that schools should act on, that is, their permission will not bring them resources they can utilize to deal with the concrete problems of their concrete schools but rather it will discharge the moral obligation to contribute to knowledge. As generations of researchers can testify, schools have rarely enthusiastically rolled out the welcome mat. Schools perceived, and rightly so, that they were entering a one-way street relationship. The researcher was crystal clear about his or her self-interests, the schools felt they were being exploited, that whatever satisfaction they might experience from allowing the researcher to do his or her thing was small recompense for what they were giving. (But it does say something positive about the appeal to altruism that many schools have given permission.)

Why is it that I have never known school people to say to a researcher: "We know what your needs are. Let us tell you what our needs are and see what you can do for us. Perhaps we can work out an exchange that would be mutually productive?" In order to adopt that approach several things have to be clear. The first, of course, is that you know what additional resources you would like to obtain for the school. The second is that you have determined the skills and interests of the researcher, neither of which may be fully (or at all) reflected in the research proposal. The third is that that determination suggests a possible match between a school need and a researcher's skills and interests. In other words, you do not look on the researcher qua researcher but as a person with diverse skills and interests you can exploit for your self-interest, someone who can do something you would like done but for whom you have neither the personnel nor the funds. As long as you see a researcher *only* as a researcher, you have blinded yourself to and enormously narrowed your perception of the diverse "resources" the researcher *may* have that can be of use to you. "What do you have that I need, and what do I have that you need"—that is a stance which facilitates *redefining* people as resources, permitting you to go beyond stereotypes and categorical thinking.

I did not give these examples as a way of saying that redefining resources—seeing people other than through the prism of labels—"solves" the brute fact of limited resources. To say or imply that would be stupid and irresponsible. But it is not stupid or irresponsible to say that we are too frequently imprisoned in and victims of the psychological set to regard the resources of an individual only in terms of what the conventional label we append to that individual suggests. That is why I expect that many readers will have regarded my proposal about teacher–parent governance of a school as outlandish. The labels *parents* and *teachers* are not associated in our minds with the knowledge and potentials to be responsible for a school. The imagery that the label *teacher* conjures up in our minds is a person in a classroom with students; whatever assets or skills we attribute to the teacher are displayed in the classroom and all other assets the teacher may have are of no interest to us. And that is also the case when we label someone as a parent. That the parent may have been a teacher, or had (or has) experience in marketing, or is or has been engaged in diverse activities in religious or other nonprofit organizations, or has a home-based business, or is a neighborhood or community activist is not revealed or suggested by the label *parent*.

Relevant here is the conception of "undermanned" and "overmanned" setting so well put forth by Roger Barker and P.V. Gump (1964) in their seminal book *Big School, Small School.* An undermanned school is one that, unlike an overmanned school, does not have sufficient *formal* resources to achieve its goals. An overmanned school may regard its resources as far from ideal, but it has discernibly more resources than the undermanned school. In his study of the two types of schools, Barker found that in the undermanned school, students and teachers engaged in activities, or were in roles, more diverse than those of teachers and students in overmanned schools. In addition, in the undermanned school there was a sense of mutuality and community among everyone that was far greater and poignant than was found in the much larger, more-staffed, overmanned school. It is not always the case that necessity is the mother of invention, but it is frequently the case. The characteristics of and pressures on the undermanned setting—whether it be a school or store or business or a large family—force one to consider redefining resources.

In the normal course of living we are not forced to redefine people as resources unless circumstances tell us that our way of labeling people obscured knowledge that prevented us from knowing that the labels we have used have mislead us. For example, I have a neighbor, Dag Pfeiffer, who 10 years ago retired from a management position in an engineering firm. Everybody should have a neighbor like him: ever ready to be of whatever help he can be, and to a mechanical idiot like me the occasions have been many. I have known him, his wife, and children for years. Four years ago he said, almost as an aside, that he was taking courses in musical composition and that he was almost finished composing a piece for a marching band. I was surprised, to say the least, and I confess that I did not look forward to hearing it when it was finished. I had trouble encompassing his composition in the imagery conjured up in my mind by the label *composer.* To make a long story short, that first composition was played by the New Haven Orchestra, and Dag continues with his composing. The point of the anecdote is that I never had occasion to take Dag's individuality seriously, by which I mean that I had never pursued the substance and range of his interests, hobbies, and talents. To me he was Dag the wonderful, decent neighbor. It never could occur to me that music had long been one of his passions. I am not accustomed to taking the life history of a neighbor! Similarly we are not accustomed to seeing students, teacher, and parents other than through labels we append them. We do not see them as individuals but as people in roles, and each role has a label that purports to tell us what the individual is entitled to be or not to be, to do or not to do.

Labels are informative, but we are unaware of how little they tell us about individuality. For example, up until three decades ago a nurse was a nurse, period. We all knew what a nurse did and what her (few hims) status was in relation to the far more elevated physician. Should nurses be *really* in charge of a hospital wing or floor? Should nurses, and only nurses, determine what nurses did? Should they be in the highest administration echelons of a hospital? Should nursing be an *autonomous* profession, not handmaidens to physicians? Should nurses be allowed to set up a non-hospital private office offering a variety of services, personal and otherwise, in regard to matters of health? Those questions would have been, and were, inconceivable or regarded as errant nonsense. To anyone knowledgeable about hospitals and nursing those questions pointed to today's transformed realities. It is a very different ballgame. How did that come about? The short answer is that nurses, particularly heads of nursing schools, redefined what they were and could be, i.e., as nurses they no longer wanted to be seen only in terms of the narrow range of knowledge and skills that the label *nurse* conjured up. The label never reflected what nurses actually did and, therefore, what they could be. Needless to say, the opposition of the medical community was strong, correctly seeing as they did that their power and authority in hospitals would be curtailed. Generally speaking, the nurses won the battle, and the medical community not only has adjusted to the new state of affairs but regards it favorably.

The preceding has been prologue to this question: What are the different ways middle and high school students can contribute to the intellectual and communal purpose of schooling? Let me ask the question more narrowly and concretely: What if every elementary school teacher had one or two of these students for 1 hour everyday and could use them in whatever ways the teacher could justify in terms of the education of those in his or her classroom? (I assume, of course, that the students would not be chosen on a random basis; there would be a selection process.) The teacher could use them to read stories to the children, or to be one-on-one, mentor-like with students who need extra help, or to supervise children in play, or to eat with and supervise children at lunchtime, or to help out with a weekly or monthly classroom newsletter.[1] Let me hasten to say that what I am suggesting has been done in more than a few schools. But this cannot be contemplated, let alone implemented, unless one sees a student as capable of being other than someone who is in a classroom "learning" with peers. That was the point of the example I gave earlier where high school students carried out a research project for a university professor who initially was aghast when the use of these students was suggested to her. To the professor the label *high school student* contraindicated using students as research collaborators. In her case necessity was the mother of risk-taking compromise. To the person who made the suggestion to the professor there was no risk; he knew the students: their interests, hobbies, and their need to do something new and meaningful. They were not "only" students; each had a distinctive individuality that could be exploited in ways that were educational for them and others.

We hear much today about providing students the opportunity to engage in community service. Behind that suggestion is the realization that as students go from the elementary to the middle to the high school many of them become increasingly bored with and turned off from *unproductive* contexts for learning. Life in school is vastly less interesting for them than life outside of school. The purpose of community service is not only to expand a student's knowledge of and experience with the "real" world but to do it in a way that gives the student a sense of growth and competence, an increased motivation to experience and learn. *But are not schools also communities to which a student can render a service that for him or her would be a context for productive learning?*

In 1978 a middle school teacher, R. Vlahakis, *and his students* wrote a book, *Kids Who Care* (Dowling College Press, Oakdale, N.Y.). In the Shoreham-Wading River Middle School approximately 50% of its 600 students spend several hours each week in a helping relationship with aged or handicapped people in several community settings. These experiences are supervised in a way that maximizes what students are doing and learning about themselves, others, and their community. In brief, this was not experience for the sake of experience. It is as heartwarming and instructive a book as one will read because it chronicles the transformations in attitude, the acquiring of new knowledge, and the intellectual stimulation it provided both to the teacher and the students. Initially, those in charge of the community sites were very reluctant for these students (average age of 12) to be in their settings, much as the college professor was reluctant to use high school students as helpers in her research. After the first year, reluctance was replaced by enthusiastic acceptance. Indeed, those in charge of the community sites wanted more students for more time. That program has continued over the years.[2] The significance of the story in that book does not lie in its redefinition and uses of students, because what the book demonstrates was demonstrated by others before and after that book, although most of these demonstrations were not published, and, to my knowledge, none that was published was authored by teachers *and* students. The significance of that book is suggested in several questions. The first question is: Why have these demonstrations remained rarities rather than spreading to many more schools? The answer is that our existing educational system is not one that encourages, facilitates, and supports such a spread. On the contrary, as I have said in earlier chapters, the existing system, far from providing incentives, rewards uniformity and makes departures from that norm a battle and dangerous, especially if they appear to contain an element of risk. The existing system is not one that learns but one that sustains conventional wisdom that, of course, frequently has the characteristics of the conventional and none of the characteristics of wisdom.

The second question, related to the first, is: Why is it so difficult for educators—although they are by no means unusual in this respect—to consider redefining resources available to them? The answer is a complex one and part of it is that there is nothing in their preparation to sensitize them to the nature and characteristics of a self-correcting system. A self-correcting system is one that cannot afford to deal with its problems by ignoring how it is defining and using its resources. The post–World War II industrial development of Japan is relevant here. At the end of the war Japanese industry was in a shambles. Within three decades it was well on its way to becoming economically dominant in the world. Central to the story was Edward Deming, an American whose expertise was in organizational systems and development. The concept of Total Quality Management was developed by Deming. What is most relevant here is that Deming's concept required (among other things) a radical redefinition of the role and resources of everyone in an organization in order to increase the number of people with a role in the self-correcting process as well as in the quality of the product. The self-correcting process did not begin after the product was finished but was in play in every step of its manufacture; and that meant giving new roles and responsibility to everyone in the organization. And while this was going on in Japan, American industry continued to operate as it always had on the assumption that the future would be a carbon copy of the past, so why change? It took a long time for American industry even to see the problem or to understand how Deming and the Japanese had taken the features of the self-correcting system and the redefinition process seriously. Even today, American industry cannot be said to have drawn the appropriate conclusions. And that is even more true in regard to our educational system in which self-correction and the redefinition of resources are alien ideas.

Anne Forester (1991a) is one of the few who has seen the relevance of Total Quality Management to the educational system. To help the reader grasp the significances of that relevance are Tables 7.1 and 7.2, in which Deming's point of view is contrasted with the conventional one. As the reader will see, these tables essentially contrast unproductive and productive contexts for learning. It will be obvious that to take Deming seriously requires a redefinition of existing resources.

I very much admire what Forester presents to us. Why, then, has what she has written gone undiscussed, unnoticed, and obviously unimplemented? My answer is no different than what I said in an earlier chapter: The existing governance system is not one primarily devoted to creating and sustaining contexts for productive learning. Just as no one in the system will argue in

(Text continues on p. 112)

TABLE 7.1.

Parallels Between Deming's 14 Points for Management and Current Trends in Education

Management	Education
1. Create constancy of purpose toward improvement of product and service, with the aim to become competitive and to stay in business, and to provide jobs.	1. Creates constancy of purpose toward improvement of service to students and the community, with the aim of enhancing learning for *ALL* students and making education relevant to their lives both in school and beyond.
2. Adopt a new philosophy. We are in a new economic age. Western management must awaken to the challenge, must learn their responsibilities, and take on leadership for a change.	2. Adopts a new philosophy. We are in an information age, and leaders in education are shifting focus on curricula and products of education to a focus on learners and their best ways of functioning. By affirming that students are effective learners and building on their strengths, teachers are creating a climate for lifelong learning in which creativity and productivity far outstrip the traditional curricula-driven model.
3. Cease dependence on inspection to achieve quality. Eliminate the need for inspection on a mass basis by building quality into the product in the first place.	3. Ceases dependence on tests and examinations to achieve quality. Eliminates the need for frequent testing by building ongoing evaluation into the teaching–learning interactions between teachers and students, students and their peers, and students with their own work. Instead of interrupting the flow of learning, the process-bound evaluation enhances it and teaches students how to examine their own work and improve it.
4. End the practice of awarding business on the basis of price tag. Instead, minimize total cost. Move toward a single supplier for any one item, on a long-term relationship of loyalty and trust.	4. Ends the practice of dwelling on the cost of quality education and looks instead for effective ways of fostering learning by using the loyalty and teamwork of a dedicated staff and the support services available in the community.

5. Improve constantly and forever the system of production and service, to improve quality and productivity, and thus constantly decrease costs.

6. Institute training on the job.

7. Institute leadership. The aim of supervision should be to help people and machines and gadgets to do a better job. Supervision and management is in need of overhaul as well as supervision of production workers.

8. Drive out fear, so that everyone may work effectively for the company.

9. Break down barriers between departments. People in research, design, sales, and production must work as a team to foresee problems of production and in use that may be encountered with the product or service.

5. Improves constantly and forever the ways of delivering services to the students by observing closely what is productive for them, how they function best, and what encourages them to excel.

6. Institutes in-house in-service training in which teachers collaborate in the same productive way their students collaborate in class working on issues and challenges that have direct relevance to their lives.

7. Institutes leadership that encourages teachers and staff to function freely; to work as a team on all levels, and that creates the same positive climate for working that teachers create in the classrooms for their students.

8. Drives out fear so that learning can flow unhampered by fear of failure, fear of reprisals, fear of ridicule, or the embarrassment of low marks. Safety to learn for student and safety to function as competent professionals for teachers are high priorities and part of the new philosophy of teaching–learning.

9. Breaks down barriers between learning disciplines and fosters writing across the curriculum, reading across the curriculum, and content-learning through projects and themes that integrate all areas of learning. It also eliminates the barriers of age, sex, and ability levels and encourages students to work in terms within their own class and with students from other classes. And it helps teachers to cooperate and network with one another by team teaching, combining classes, drawing an entire school into a project or collaborating with other schools.

(continued)

TABLE 7.1. (*continued*)

Management	Education
10. Eliminate slogans, exhortations, and targets for the work force asking for zero defects and new levels of productivity. Such exhortations only create adversarial relationships, as the bulk of the causes of low quality and low productivity belong to the system and thus lie beyond the powers of the work force.	10. Eliminates lectures and exhortations about doing quality work that is free of mistakes. Such lectures only intimidate and antagonize students as few of them are shown appropriate models of what constitutes quality work and fewer still have been invited to discuss the rationale for doing good work and to agree upon standards of quality.
11a. Eliminate work standards (quotas) on the factory floor. Substitute leadership.	11a. Eliminates assignment quotas and substitutes leadership in the classroom whereby the teacher and fellow students model learning behaviors, the production of writing, steps in research and, above all, enthusiasm for learning and inquiry.
11b. Eliminate management by objective. Eliminate management by numbers, numerical goals. Substitute leadership.	11b. Eliminates learning objectives that suggest limited goals for learning and substitutes leadership in exploring new ways of extracting, analyzing and presenting material. Curiosity, the drive to know, to get accurate information and to present it in inter-esting ways become the energy that fuels learning.
12a. Remove barriers that rob the hourly worker of his right to pride of workmanship. The responsibility of supervisors must be changed from sheer numbers to quality.	12a. Remove barriers that rob students of their right to pride in their work. Instead of evaluating work in terms of quantity and numbers of jobs completed, teachers encourage students to polish their writing to its fullest luster, to delve into questions of science or mathematics to their fullest and to follow a project to its conclusion based on the students' judgment, not a time or curriculum restraint.
12b. Remove barriers that rob people in management and in engineering of their right to pride of workmanship. This means, inter alia, abolishment of the annual merit rating and of management by objective.	12b. Removes barriers that rob teachers and principals of professional pride. Instead of setting specific objectives for the year, teachers and principals interact as autonomous, collaborating professionals.

13. Institute a vigorous program of education and self-improvement.

13. Institutes a vigorous program of overall self-improvement that includes physical, social, aesthetic, and creative development along with intellectual growth. In the interactive, collaborative climate of the classroom teachers and students are co-learners who grow and develop together on all levels.

14. Put everybody in the company to work to accomplish the transformation. The transformation is everybody's job.

14. Puts everyone in the school to work on creating a climate that transforms education. The climate that empowers students to become effective, independent learners includes everyone in the school. From the support staff to the principal, everyone is collaborating in creating a learning community.

Source: Forester, Anne D. "An Examination of Parallels Between Deming's Model for Transforming Industry and Current Trends in Education." Paper presented at the National Learning Foundation's TQE/TQM Seminar, Washington, D.C., October 10, 1991.

TABLE 7.2.

Using a Management Model to Compare Teaching Styles

The Boss Teacher	The Lead Teacher
Decides what will be taught and how it will be learned	Sets the framework for learning but leaves room for options
Keeps strict control of all aspects of the classroom	Encourages students to make choices about their learning
Decides on the rules and on how to enforce them	Discusses reasons for rules and asks for student' input to formulate and enforce those rules
Keeps a strong focus on the curriculum to shape lessons and is more concerned with the *what* of learning than the *how*	Observes learners and their needs and interests to foster learning that fulfills students' needs as well as curriculum requirements
Tends to use the lecture format to convey information	Models the skills to be learned and uses experimental, hands-on work
Relies heavily on Cazden's (1988) IRE model-teacher Initiation, student **R**esponse, teacher **E**valuation	Engages students in discussions about the relevance and quality of work undertaken in class and makes information sharing reciprocal
Tries to have all students work on the same job at the same time	Offers choices that fit the work to students' interests, abilities, maturity, and experience
Generally has students work by themselves	Often uses teamwork and cooperative learning
Generally is the chief information giver and initiator of jobs, themes, or projects	Encourages students to share information and to initiate projects
Relies on outside motivation—grades, praise—to urge students to work hard	Relies on the inner motivation of students to excel and trusts them to work to the best of their abilities
Sees education as serious business that needs to be shaped by a knowledgeable leader—the teacher	Sees learning as exciting, as fun, and as arising from students' own needs and curiosity stimulated by interesting work
Generally feels that students must be closely supervised to ensure that they do the work	Trusts students to work in their own ways and at their own pace

Relies largely on tests, work sheets, and examinations to evaluate students' progress	Uses informal observation and ongoing anecdotal records to evaluate students' progress and to enrich information derived from examinations
Generally sees record keeping and evaluation as the teacher's job	Has students keep many of the records and uses their self-evaluations to augment teacher observation
Holds the power in the classroom	Empowers students to work freely on academic tasks while observing social rules that have been established cooperatively
Focuses on the end product of learning	Focuses on the process of learning
Manages the curriculum	Manages people

Derived from William Glasser's "The Quality School: What Motivates the Arts?" *Phi Delta Kappan*, Feb. 1990: 424–435.
Source: Forester, Anne D., and Margaret Reinhard. *On the Move—Teaching the Learners' Way in Grades 4–7.* Winnipeg, Canada: Peguis Publishers, 1991, pp. 40–41.

favor of crime, illness, and misery, they will in the abstract not argue in favor of unproductive contexts for learning. Everybody, again in the abstract, is in favor of productive contexts, but when faced, as they would be if they took Forester's comparisons seriously, with how the roles and resources of everyone in and related to the school would undergo redefinition, they conclude that it would be easier to climb Mt. Everest than to change a system that has a plethora of disincentives against and a virtual absence of incentives for change.

My proposals for school governance assume that the parents and teachers of a school accept the responsibility to create and sustain contexts for productive learning for *everyone*. I would expect that they would feel free to consider any idea, project, or process that gave promise of furthering the overarching purpose of schooling, and that means they would not summarily dismiss the use of middle and high school students in the elementary school because it would be such a departure from current practice. Their responsibility comes with the authority to decide what their school is and what they want it to be. They are accountable and, therefore, they are obligated to ask questions about any problem with which they are faced: What can we do to prevent the problem from occurring again? What needs to change? Do we have the resources to implement the change? Are there resources in or out of the school that might be available to us to help us to make the change? The last question does not assume that an outside resource will only be obtainable by paying for it, although each school will have some funds to use for such a purpose. One should not define a resource as that which you pay for and therefore control, and if you cannot pay for it you cannot have it. One should begin by asking: Given what we need is there someone in the community who can help us meet that need and whose self-interest will dispose the person to give some time to help us meet that need without asking compensation? For example, a number of years ago I made it my business to ask each member of the Yale faculty whom I knew or met this question: Have you ever been asked by anyone in any New Haven school to consult with them because someone thought that you had knowledge and skills that would be helpful to them? I also asked if in response to such a request that faculty member would come to such a meeting. None of the 30 or so faculty I talked with had ever received such a request. Every one of them said something like the following: "I do not know how I could be helpful, but if someone thought I could be helpful of course I would go, if only to satisfy my curiosity."

Let us now look at another facet of the definition and utilization of resources. Here is how I have expressed it on several occasions in meetings with the faculty of a school.

I am going to put to you some questions I would like you to ponder for several minutes. Really, it is one question with several variants. The first question is, what information, skills, hobbies, interests do you have that are or may be relevant to the education of children—not necessarily relevant to the particular age group you happen to be teaching but to some students somewhere in the school system. Some of you are married so I ask you also to think about the question in regard to your spouses. Is there anything they know, or have done, or are doing that would be educationally and intellectually instructive to some groups of students? The final question is similar but concerns the parents of your students. They may be parents of children you are now teaching or others you happen to know.

Please do not be concerned with the practical problem of whether the particular "resources" you and others possess can be made available for educational purposes. Assume that there is no practical problem. What are the special resources potentially available to you, resources that can have payoff for students? Please take a piece of paper and simply list what those resources are.

Several things were noteworthy about the reactions and responses of the groups to whom I put the questions. The first was from those teachers who had strong, long-standing skills, hobbies, or interests that they in no way utilized in their classrooms or who never thought that what they possessed could be utilized elsewhere. The best example was the teacher who only in discussion revealed that he had a large stamp collection that he had never considered relevant to social studies, geography, history, or arithmetic. Another example was the teacher who had a voluminous collection of photographs and newspaper accounts of Italian immigrants arriving at Ellis Island. It was not on her list of personal resources because it never occurred to her that it could have educational value for others. Generally speaking, the skills, interests, and hobbies of teachers were in a psychological world unrelated to that of children in classrooms.

The second interesting reaction had to do with spouses. Here, too, but to a lesser degree than with the teachers' personal resources, the educational relevance of what spouses did tended to be ignored on the lists of teachers. For example, the wife of one math teacher was the chief nurse in the operating room of the local hospital; this information came out in discussion, but the teacher had great difficulty justifying its potential in instruction. One husband was a home builder, but his teaching wife had not listed this information and strenuously resisted my suggestion that building homes was a fruitful means of illustrating the significance of geometry, physics, economics,

and more. Then there was the husband whose wife had not listed his occu-
pation: owner of a large, regional private garbage-collecting business. When
this came out in discussion, I did not have to say anything because several
teachers in the group immediately saw the relevance of his business to the
chemistry, biology, economics, and quandaries of waste disposal. I bless the
teacher in that group who had the courage to ask: "I really have long been
curious about how human urine and feces are disposed of in a spaceship,
especially the ones that stay in outer space for weeks or months." So was I
and everybody else in that room.

The third noteworthy reaction was reflected in the fact that parents as
resources appeared infrequently on lists. If I had to guess, I would say that
three-quarters of the teachers knew little or nothing about parental occupa-
tions, interests, or hobbies. If I limited myself to high school teachers, the per-
centage would be nearer 90 percent.

The point of the exercise was to indicate that there are resources potentially available and, if available, quite relevant to educational purposes, to teachers. That was the obvious point. A less obvious one was that even if those
resources were available, their utilization would be difficult given the way
schools and school days are organized. It is unfair to say that schools are
organized like an assembly line in a car factory. But it is not unfair to say that
they are organized around and wedded to such narrow conception of curriculum as to make departures from routine require a degree of courage and
innovativeness for which educational medals of honor should be given.

I do not believe that educators are uncreative and unimaginative but
rather that those characteristics are neither nurtured nor reinforced in preparatory programs or schools. Beginning in preparatory programs and continuing into their socialization as independent practitioners, they learn a rigid
conception of the school day, week, month, and year, one that expresses a routine as ludicrous as the travel schedule caricatured in the title of the movie
If It's Tuesday, We Must Be In Belgium. We should remember, however, that
a caricature is a reflection of reality; it has force for us to the degree that it
distorts reality in order to emphasize one or several significant facets of it.
The isolation of teachers and their students in an encapsulated physical space
instills in them, subtly but pervasively, the narrowest of conceptions of who
and what are educational resources, potential or actual. When, as in the exercise in which I engaged them, educators find redefining resources a difficult
process and imagining ways of using them an exercise in futile fantasy, it should
occasion no surprise. Creativity, imaginativeness, and spontaneity in individuals are almost always functions of present or past contexts for these characteristics. To blame educators is to blame the victim.

There was one more not so obvious point to the exercise. It is less a point
than a predictable consequence that teachers (on their own) found surpris-

ing. *Teachers knew amazingly little about their colleagues' or colleagues' spouses' interests, skills, and hobbies. The lack of collegiality in intellectual–educational issues was rivaled by a similar lack of personal collegiality.* Both lacks have no simple explanation, but to an undetermined (and I would say large) extent, they reflect a style of school governance that tends to make school personnel strangers to each other. And if strangers is too strong a word, I will accept any word or phrase that conveys the superficiality of relationships among personnel in a school. Of course there are exceptions. But that is what they are: exceptions.

I trust that what I have said will not be interpreted as suggesting that the redefinition of resources "solves" the fact of limited resources. The examples I presented were intended to emphasize that the process of redefining resources increases the pool of resources *potentially* available for this or that purpose. But for that process to be contemplated, let alone pursued in action, is not possible in an organization so rigidly structured, so pressured by perceived time constraints, so preoccupied with its internal workings as to blot out consideration of the possibilities of redefining resources. Few things contribute more to this state of affairs than a governance structure wedded to and reinforcing of what years ago I called the "disease of professionalism": Professionals, *not only in education,* define problems in a way so as to insure that more professionals will be needed, thus making limited resources even more limited. I can assure the reader that I respect what a highly trained professional knows and can do. However, when it is perfectly obvious that the number of professionals is and will be insufficient to deal with the number and complexity of problems for which those professionals are appropriate, are we not obligated to ask if there are others who *may* be able in *some* way to be of *some* help with those problems. Are we justified only to moan and wail about insufficient resources? Are we justified in blaming a niggardly society, ignoring as that criticism does the vast disparity between the number of professionals and the number of individuals who need help? Are we justified in accepting a state of affairs in which the time and services of professionals are rationed with the result that the quality of their services is diluted? Are we justified in clinging to the myth of unlimited resources—that there is no social problem intractable to "solution" if there is the national will and the appropriate funding to eliminate the problem?

Few readers will be acquainted with the Industrial Areas Foundation (IAF), which was created years ago by Saul Alinsky (1992), who was, to say the least, an original thinker and an effective community organizer. Today the IAF is most active in the poorest areas in the cities of the Southwest and California. Here are some basic facts about how an organizer comes onto the scene.

1. Local churches, constituting an Interfaith Council, garner the funds to pay for 2 years of an organizer's salary.
2. The IAF selects an organizer who has gone through an intensive training centering on the rationale and tactics of community organizing.
3. The "iron rule" of IAF is made explicit: You do not do for someone what that person can do for him- or herself.

The usual imagery conjured up by the label "organizers" is misleading here.

The organizer begins with "house meetings," which are far more often than not a one-on-one meeting in a person's home. It is not at all unusual that in the first year the organizer will have done nothing but seek and have *hundreds* of house meetings. The sole purpose of these meetings is to allow the person to voice what is wrong with or absent from that part of the community where the person lives. As one organizer said to me, "In these communities there are three groups: those with high income, those with low income, and those with no income. We work with those in parts two and three." In addition to determining what is wrong and absent, the organizer seeks to determine whether the person is or may be willing to meet with and work with others who have similar grievances. The role of the organizer is a nondirective one. But in addition to listening the organizer is on a talent hunt, i.e., forming preliminary judgments about which people seem to have leadership characteristics plus a willingness to participate in collective actions. At some point in the process groups of individuals meet and, together with the Interfaith Council, try to determine which specific grievance stands the best chance of being remedied by an initial community action. That is an important decision because if the community action is successful it gives citizens a basis for expecting that future actions will further decrease their sense of powerlessness, i.e., success is empowering. That initial decision is made after several questions have been confronted and answered. What data do we need to substantiate that our grievance is justified? Where can we get that data? Who will get it? In regard to each of these questions the organizer plays a role, but he or she does not play the role of researcher, that becomes the responsibility of the group and of emerging indigenous leaders. It is not the organizer who talks for the group, or is the spokesperson who arranges meetings with local officialdom, business, or banking organizations. The "iron rule" is fundamental. Let me illustrate this by a personal experience.

Since 1990 I have been on an advisory committee to Dr. Paul Heckman, who has been spearheading an effort to change and improve schools in Tucson's poorest Hispanic neighborhoods. I shall have more to say about Dr. Heckman on later pages of this chapter. Suffice it to say here that on my first visit to one of these schools there were representatives of the Pima County

Interfaith Council. All but one of them was articulate in expressing their views of the inadequacies of the school and the community in which it was embedded. At each subsequent visit the Interfaith Council representatives were present at meetings, including one person who rarely said anything. He appeared to be a laid-back person but his vigilant attentiveness was obvious. When on those rare occasions he said something, I made the judgment that behind that business-like facade was a very smart and well-educated person. During coffee breaks we sometimes chitchatted, but neither of us sought to learn anything about the other. All I knew was that in some way he was connected with the Interfaith Council, which had accomplished much for the poor, ignored, heretofore powerless citizens of south Tucson. His name was Frank Pearson, and he was the IAF organizer. Clearly, all of his actions were consistent with the iron rule. It was not that he was content to be in the background, but that he *had to be there* if his organizing efforts were to be judged successful.

I said that the organizer was always on a talent hunt. He did not judge people by whether they could talk English, or that they lived in dilapidated, shack-like homes, or that they appeared to have given up hope that they could do anything that would make a difference in their lives or community, or that they were mothers and fathers resigned to being passive about the fates of their children in a neighborhood of drugs, violence, and drink, or that they clung desperately to their churches as the sole sources of solace in an indifferent world. What the organizer did was to give them a platform to voice grievance and despair, to listen sympathetically and respectfully to what they had to say, and to suggest (not to promise) that by collective action with others who felt the same way *maybe* something beneficial might be accomplished. And by bringing them together with others who felt just as hopeless or angry there emerged individuals with the qualities of initiative, planning, inventiveness, boldness, and courage. *The IAF organizing process is one that seeks to create and sustain contexts of productive learning for people who had never experienced that kind of context. The organizer starts with where the individual is, not with their obvious deficits but with their assets, actual or potential, and it is a process not unduly constrained by the pressure of time.* The organizer builds on the assets. More correctly, the people become the crucible in which individuals begin to redefine themselves and others, and to locate and use other resources about which they had known nothing or that they had regarded as utterly inaccessible to them. They were learning in a context that made them willingly want to learn and experience more.

My sole purpose in discussing the IAF was to emphasize how central to its rationale and tactics is the redefinition of people as resources. That its achievements have been many is a conclusion warranted by numerous publications (e.g., Rogers, 1990; Watriss, 1990). What is the significance of the rationale for schools, a question that the IAF has in recent years begun to address? The most compelling answer is provided by Dr. Paul Heckman's project in several south Tucson elementary schools, initiated in 1990. Although the conceptions undergirding his efforts are similar to those of IAF, they were derived independently from his long experience in diverse roles in schools. That is an important point because he was painfully aware that however successful the redefinition process and alterations in power relationships may be in a school, their impact on students and teachers depended on achieving clarity and consistency about the differences between productive and unproductive contexts for learning. In organizing a community the IAF is crystal clear that the community has to come to have specific, concrete, attainable goals. What, Dr. Heckman asked, was the goal of changing schools? To give teachers and parents more authority and power? To increase scores on achievement tests? To change the curriculum? To find new ways to motivate students? To obtain and better use technology in the classroom? For Dr. Heckman those are relatively concrete goals, but they missed the point of dealing with the practical implications of the criteria for productive contexts of learning. To put it negatively, why do classrooms and schools meet almost all of the criteria of contexts for unproductive learning? You cannot answer a question you do not ask of yourself. For example, on countless occasions over the years I have asked teachers this question: When you look back at your public school days can you identify those times, which may be few or many, when you were doing or learning something that was interesting, stimulating, and, so to speak, turned you on because in some way you had a sense of discovery, of learning something about yourself and/or the world that made you want to learn more? That is to say, it made personal sense to you? With few exceptions teachers were somewhat chagrined at the difficulty they had coming up with instances. I have put the same question to high school students. Again there were a few exceptions. Almost all of the rest looked at me as if to say, "You are an old man who obviously doesn't know beans from students and schools." The idea that schools are places where what you learn has or should have *some* personal, motivating, curiosity-arousing, question-asking consequences is an alien one to the bulk of students. In response to one group of students, I said, "Are you trying to tell me that schools are places where you *learn,* you do not *do,* you *absorb* what you are told to absorb, and what you *may want to learn* you have to keep to yourself?" They looked at me as if to say, "Maybe this old man is not as kooky as his first question indicated."

I was well past midlife when the obvious penetrated my head: schools, unknowingly of course, were contexts for unproductive learning. Dr. Heckman did not have to wait to midlife to see the obvious. It is beyond my purposes to describe in detail his approach to and work in several of the schools in Tucson's Hispanic neighborhoods. The interested reader should consult *The*

Courage to Change (1995), which is an account by teachers in one of the schools of how they changed and why. Montera's (1996) recently completed study of the first 4 years of the project is similarly instructive and important. Let me briefly list the salient features of the project.

1. What Heckman calls the "reinventing school process" requires that the teachers, parents, and other community stakeholders be given the opportunity to decide what kind of a school they want and, there-fore, take responsibility for it. Dr. Heckman studiously avoided telling them the kind of school he hoped they would create. *It took well over a year for them to disabuse themselves of the expectation that the project staff was in the school to get consent to create their kind of a school.*
2. Teachers met for 3 continuous hours each week in "dialogue" sessions to talk, argue, plan, and even "dream" about what changes they could agree to. Dr. Heckman or a member of his staff was at each meeting, not to direct the discussion, but to serve as a sounding board for ideas, to remind them that whatever they decided to do had to be developed and "owned" by them, that they need not feel they were prisoners of the existing state of affairs.
3. Over a period of 6 years teachers changed their perceptions of students in that by virtue of changes that were instituted they understood that productive learning requires that you start with where the student is, where he or she comes from, etc. That did not happen quickly because, as the teachers acknowledged, they were trained to direct the attention of students to a predetermined, calendar-driven curriculum. They feared that if you started with where the student is, it would be difficult, if not impossible, to help them learn that they "needed" to know, and those poor Hispanic students "needed" to learn a great deal. That these students had already learned a great deal outside of school, that they were embedded in a family-religious-neighborhood culture that was in distinctive ways coherent and supportive, that they were not disposed to reject that culture or to create a gulf between them and their parents, that they had assets for living and learning in that culture—it took a long time for teachers to change their highly overlearned conceptions and perceptions of these students, but when they did they realized how and why they and the students had benefited.
4. The same kind of change occurred in regard to how teachers saw parents with whom they had begun to meet and interact in other than superficial ways. They were used to complaining that parents were not supportive or even interested in what a child was "doing" in school: They did not come to parent–teacher nights; they did not fol-

low through with what teachers told them to do; they were ambitious neither for themselves nor their children.[3] What teachers came to know was the polar opposite of the attitudes with which they had started.

5. The school system did not seek out Dr. Heckman; he sought the system out to gain permission to test his ideas. When it was apparent that the project was, so to speak, paying off, the system made no effort to encourage Dr. Heckman to take on other schools; Dr. Heckman again was the seeker. The existence of the project is fragile, depending as it does on one most unusual district supervisor (Elaine Rice), who essentially protects the project from the system's insensitivities, willed ignorance, and senseless rules, regulations, and directives. The school system is incapable of learning, of self-correction, and of voluntary change. Its goal is uniformity, and its logo is "No good deed goes unpunished or is worthy of recognition and spread. We will act if forced to. We prefer to stand still and be safe rather than to act, unless, of course, it is guaranteed that success will be the outcome." I am being neither snide nor contemptuous. There are no villains in the sense that those who administer the system got together and decided to create and sustain a system that is unproductive. If there were villains in the usual meaning of that word, changing schools would not be as overwhelmingly difficult as it is. They are unaware that they have accepted and are part of the system that is constantly reinventing flat tires.

This chapter turned out to be much longer than I anticipated. My justification is that transforming schools will never happen unless: (1) We become more clear about the differences between contexts for productive and unproductive learning; and (2) We reexamine our accustomed way of using labels and defining resources.

I will relate a story that serves as prologue for the following chapters. It is about a meeting in one of the south Tucson schools. Parents, teachers, and members of the advisory board were participants. The meeting followed immediately after students had exhibited to us a project they had completed in small groups. We were reviewing what we had seen. In the middle of the conversation one of the parents interrupted the discussion and in a voice tinged with plaintiveness and anger said, "Why can't these kids stay in this school for the next 2 or 3 years instead of going to the middle school where my other children are and where they are unhappy and are learning nothing?" That emboldened the other parents to say similar things. That fear was of no small concern to Dr. Heckman. It was of no concern to those in the administrative hierarchy. How could they be concerned when they knew little or nothing about and had never visited these schools? I shall be generous and assume they knew somewhat more than I think they did. If so, from my standpoint that is kin to compounding a felony. But, as I have said too many times, school systems are almost totally incapable of learning.

NOTES

[1]On a number of occasions I have asked individual teachers to come up with suggestions about how upper school students could be used in their classrooms. Some teachers found my question difficult to answer, i.e., it was for them a strange question. There were other teachers who found the question intriguing and it stimulated them to come up with suggestions that had never occurred to me and are too numerous to discuss here. One teacher said, "I read a book about the one-room schoolhouse and I was truly surprised how the teacher *had* to use older children in different ways as teacher aides. My first reaction when I read the book was that it would take pressure off of me to be all things to all students. But then I realized that the older students would be learning a lot." (emphasis hers)

[2]The book by Mr. Vlahakis and his students is no longer available and is not likely to be in many libraries. I learned about the book years ago when on several occasions I visited the school. With Mr. Vlahakis' permission I excerpted a fair amount of that book in my 1993 book, *You Are Thinking of Teaching?*

[3]What I am relating here is taken from Heckman and Montera. I got to know the teachers and some of the parents both in informal and formal meetings. What Heckman and Montera report in no way differs from what I observed and learned. My visits were among the most inspiring I have ever had in schools, and I am not noted for my optimism about school change. When I agreed to be on the project's advisory committee I did not expect to be on it long because I assumed that a point would come when it would be clear that this project would be another well-intentioned fiasco, or if not a fiasco, one whose accomplishments did not justify my continued involvement. I agreed to serve because I had known Paul Heckman when he was a graduate student of John Goodlad at UCLA and given my respect for John Goodlad I was positively inclined. That Arizona in general, and Tucson in particular, are among the most beautiful places on earth was a secondary but very important consideration.

C H A P T E R

Beyond the Classroom

What meaning do we intend when we say that a student *learns?* Clearly, we do not mean that a student learns in a social vacuum. We take for granted that by learning we mean that there are transactions of diverse sorts between the student and an adult or, as in cooperative learning, between other students. And we also take for granted that the learner and teacher are not only known to each other but that there also is an explicit and implicit "contract" between them. What is the contract? The teacher will do his or her best to present ideas and questions in a clear way and to be sensitive to when a student does not understand, or misinterprets, or in some ways gets things "wrong." The teacher is expected to determine where the problem is and to help the student see where he or she screwed up, and to do this in a way that does not make the student feel stupid, ashamed, or a failure. We do not expect the teacher to be fulfilling his or her side of the contract by saying curtly, "You got it wrong, try again." We would be more approving if the teacher graciously said, "You got it wrong. Why don't you look over what you did and see where you went off the track. If you still get it wrong, you and I will figure out where and why you went wrong." We expect the teacher to respect the student's effort and feelings not as a matter only of courtesy but as a reflection of how a teacher understands that what he or she does or says is part of the context of learning, a part that can be positive or negative for how the student experiences learning. From the

122

student's standpoint what a teacher does or says is never neutral in its consequences, it is a difference that makes a difference. We can sum all of this up by saying that we expect the teacher to know how to adjust his or her words, tactics, and approach to the individuality of the student. That is a complicated, indeed awesome, task to perform well. But that is the contract.

For the student the contract has several features. The first is that he or she will be attentive, cooperative, and motivated. The second is that the student feels psychologically safe in the sense that he or she expects that the teacher knows and understands him or her, and can be expected to be helpful when the student is having difficulty, asks for guidance, support, and reassurance. Whether the student is having a problem or not, the student expects an appropriate recognition for the quantity and quality of this work. The student expects that he or she knows and respects the teacher the way the student feels the teacher knows or respects him or her. *The contract assumes that teacher and student know each other and that **know** means much more than what is characteristic of superficial interpersonal relationships where thoughts and feelings remain largely unexpressed and private. That kind of knowing is virtually impossible in a middle school that is at least twice the size of an elementary school or in a high school that is at least twice the size of a middle school and often up to three or four times larger.* An elementary school teacher may have 25 (or more) students, but the teacher is with those students almost all of each school day. A middle or high school teacher may have five classes, each of which the teacher sees for 45 minutes each day. The teacher teaches a particular subject matter and does not have the "luxury" of being with those students other than in his or her classroom and in regard only to that particular subject matter. And, of course, because the teacher is under pressure to cover a particular curriculum, the teacher regards each class hour as one in which some aspect or part of the curriculum must be covered and "learned" by the students. The reader is probably familiar with what is called the page 72 syndrome: "By October 15 we must be up to page 72 in the textbook."

These words are being written at a time when school budgets are being cut and class size increased. I have yet to talk with teachers, especially in our urban schools, who are not bitter about class size increase. That does not mean that teachers were happy with the size of earlier classes, especially middle and high school teachers. Even before the increase, middle and high school teachers would readily admit in private conversation that there was no way they could get to know most of their students, if by *know* was meant that they had anything resembling what would be a personal relationship. Not an intimate relationship, to be sure, but one in which student and teacher each had an understanding of or interest in each other, i.e., they were not two people whose interactions were fleeting, superficial, and formally routine and correct.

As I have said earlier, in the middle and high school years student disinterest and boredom markedly increase. What would require explanation would be if that was not the case. This is not only because of the size of the school and classroom, or the way the school day is chopped up, or the consequences of the pressure to adhere to a calendar-driven curriculum, but because of the students' perception that what they are required to learn has no personal significance for them and that perception cannot, must not, be a subject for discussion.

This increase has more than one source. It would be unfair to place blame wholly on teachers and schools, but it is not unfair to say that the single most potent source is student perception that middle and high schools are impersonal, unstimulating, and rivet on subject matter that, for the student, has no connection to personal experience, leading the student to conclude that subject matter is a form of medicine for a condition he or she cannot identify and does not feel he or she has. The attitudes of Mr. Holland's students had diverse sources but, as the movie portrays, Mr. Holland and that high school played a major role. The most recent study documenting pervasive student disengagement is by Steinberg, Brown, and Dornbusch (1996). The authors attribute the disengagement almost exclusively to lack of parental interest, supervision, and stimulation (e.g., Steinberg, 1996). That is a gross oversimplification that I do not wish to deal with here except to say that for a period of years I spent a lot of time in inner city schools observing kindergartners and first and second graders. Whereas they began school with buoyancy, enthusiasm, and curiosity, by the end of the second grade the beginnings of disengagement were plain to see. Few had been "hooked." Of course the role of parents is crucial. But in none of the schools did the educators seriously, sincerely, persistently, creatively seek to make parents interested *and* accountable.

There are, unfortunately, many children who learn that it is dangerous, or unrewarding, or futile to expect that their parents are capable of discussing with them issues, opinions, and questions about their relationships. That is precisely the way many middle and high school students perceive their teachers: demanding, controlling, obsessed with subject matter, and basically not interested in what students "really" think and feel. It is asking too much of students to expect that they could understand that both they and teachers are victims of the "system" and their victimization manifests itself differently. But there is another factor: If students are sure of anything it is that life in school bears little relationship to life as they see or experience it outside of school. About World War I it was said, "How can you keep them down on the farm once they have seen Paree?" For too many middle and high school students school is the farm and life away from it is Paree.

It is not happenstance that the bulk of reform efforts have been in elementary schools that, compared to middle and high schools, are models of organizational simplicity. Middle and high schools are bureaucratic, factory-like organizations that manifest all of the interpersonal, turf, decision-making, and planning-style problems of that type of organization. The concentration of reform efforts on the elementary school is always justified by the superiority of the preventive over the repair orientation, just as Headstart was and is justified by its goal to prevent the appearance of problems in the elementary school. Put it this way: Headstart is an effort to prevent children from catching the viruses of academic failure and low motivation in the early school years, i.e., Headstart is a form of inoculation against academic illnesses. No one disputes that for too many students the transitions to middle and high school bring in their wake a plethora of academic-interpersonal-social-motivational problems. Those problems have more than one source but one source certainly is that these schools create and sustain *unproductive* contexts of learning, a fact very well illustrated by the film *Mr. Holland's Opus* I discussed in Chapter 3. So, if reformers have tended to bypass these schools—and where they have not their accomplishments have been less than modest—it is because they know that implementing and sustaining change in these schools is an exercise in futility.[1] That does not mean that none of these schools can be appropriately and discernibly changed but that to change even *one* of these schools requires years and special circumstances that border on the unique and for all practical purposes cannot be replicated.

What if I told the reader that there is a middle school that almost from its inception attempted to create and sustain contexts of productive learning for students and teachers? And what if I went on to say that the change effort was spearheaded by several members of a college of education faculty who, wonder of wonders, persisted in sustaining that effort for 17 years, despite a litany of obstacles and frustrations emanating more from the school system than from the school itself? I could also tell the reader that although it has been and still is a very unusual middle school for students, teachers, and parents (who play a very important role), as well as for many teacher interns from the college, the continuation of the school–college collaboration is, today, very problematic because the decision for continuation rests with "higher ups" in the system who have no idea whatsoever about what is distinctive about the school and are pressuring the college participants to leave the school and take on another school that has caused the system much grief, i.e., go do your magic elsewhere, although by "do" they are not referring to 5 or 10 years, let alone 17 years. They really mean magic; that reflects the depth of their understanding about what is involved in changing a complicated, very troubled school.

The story to which I make reference has been told by Trubowitz and Longo (1997) and which is briefly discussed in my interview with them at the beginning of this book. What conclusions should we draw from their detailed story? We are justified in concluding that special people in special circumstances with special resources can reform a school, in this case keeping the school from becoming what most middle schools are. We are also justified in concluding that to accomplish this is a *continuous* uphill battle in which the major enemy is truly the way in which the system (not the school) is governed. And we are justified in concluding that without the support *and* participation of parents the reform efforts would have been aborted long ago. The story does *not* justify the conclusion that we have been provided with an "answer" for changing middle and high schools. What the story illuminates is that the system qua system is simply not geared to create and sustain productive contexts of learning. It is a system that guarantees—and I do mean *guarantees*—that for the bulk of students and teachers the middle and high school years will be spent in unproductive contexts. To expect otherwise is both illusory and dangerous; illusory because it denies the realities of those school years for students and teachers, and dangerous because it contributes to societal instability by impoverishing the minds, personality, and horizons of everyone in these schools. Education refers to the process of "getting out" of somebody that which he or she possesses or needs to possess. Education is not a process for filling empty vessels as if one vessel is like every other vessel. Education, in its root sense, is a process for determining the nature and dimensions of individuality so as to exploit it, not ignore or blunt it. We, I assume, will always fall short of the mark. To fall short of the mark is no sin. Not to take aim at the mark, to deny that there is or should be a mark, to be unable or unwilling to face up to the brute fact that your aim is getting worse rather than better, to resign yourself to accepting what is and thereby avoiding the imperative to change—together these border on the sinful, metaphorically speaking.

I agree with those who have said that no middle or high school should have more than 500 students. Why not 600 or 700? The answer is that we really do not know because in and of itself size must depend on what the overarching purpose, when taken seriously, will require. When, as is presently the case, the overarching purpose is not taken seriously, schools will be as self-defeatingly large as they are. Although reduced size can have certain desirable effects, as Barker's (1964) work demonstrates, it does not follow as night follows day that the overarching purpose is being achieved. In itself size is a frail reed on which to place high expectations. So how might we think about secondary schools *and* the overarching purpose?

For the reader to grapple with that question, it is necessary that you perform a very difficult task: Deliberately to put aside what you know about how these schools are organized and governed. Begin by imagining that there is a new secondary school, in the fall it will take in several hundred students, and the organization and governance of the school is, so to speak, up for grabs. I can assure the reader from personal experience that it is extraordinarily difficult to avoid thinking about what can and should be except in terms of the ways we have been socialized to think about the way things are. But that is what the reader must try to avoid. I emphasize that because I anticipate that many readers will find my proposals strange, or outrageous, the stuff of fantasy, and totally impractical.

The relationship between author and reader bears resemblance to that between teacher and student. I think I have something to say, to teach, something I believe to be of importance to you and our world. You are reading this book in the hope that you *may* learn something relevant to your interests. The problem is that I do not know where you are coming from, what your interests are, and how wide is the gulf between where you and I are. Because of my advanced age I have been struggling for years with the differences between what is productive and unproductive, between what is and what might or should be. As an author I am not in the position of a classroom teacher who has the opportunity to determine a student's individuality. I am more like the teacher I am criticizing in that I am teaching a "whole class," not individuals. I do not have the opportunity to start where you are and to help you see the problem in a different light. I would prefer, consistent with what I have said earlier, not to pour into or to present to you a variety of ideas and suggestions and to say, "Here is the way you should think, here is what you should do." The virtues of serious reading are many, but it has its limitations and one of them is that readers, like too many students, are unable to engage the author-teacher in meaningful discussion. Absent that engagement, the author has no way of knowing whether he or she has been comprehended, how wide the gulf is, and how the author (like me) could have done a better job. There is one thing about which I as author felt secure: My proposals will not—indeed should not—receive ready assent. And one source of resistance to my proposals will be the difficulty readers will have thinking other than in terms of what secondary schools are today. I ask less for assent than for the serious recognition about contexts of learning and *that* lack of seriousness can no longer be tolerated in a society (and world) that has changed so dramatically in the post–World War II era (Sarason, 1996a).

My first proposal is that we not think in terms of courses but rather in terms of a menu of projects, the large majority of which would require the student to leave the classroom and even his or her school to accomplish the goals of the project. The student would decide whether to carry out the project alone or with three or four other students. Before asking the student to choose from the menu there would be extensive discussion about why the decision should be that of the student, i.e., why that responsibility derives from what we know about productive learning; and the factors that should be considered in deciding whether to work alone or in a small group. Understanding the nature of contexts of productive learning will not be foreign to students; in their own ways and in differing degrees their experience has permitted them to differentiate between passive, impersonal learning and active, personally meaningful learning. They are not theoreticians or conceptualizers of productive learning, and I am not proposing to make them such, but I am saying that they have long been confronting in the home and in the school, and in very concrete ways, the difference between *having* to do or learn what others say is "good" for them and *wanting* to learn what *they* want to learn. If that is a difference they have already experienced, what they need to discuss and learn is why that kind of conflict is inevitable because it is ridiculous in the extreme to expect teachers and parents to in effect say to children, "Do only what *you* want to do. We have no right to say what *we* think you should or must do." To expect that parents and teachers can or should keep their values in check is to expect the impossible. Just as parents and teachers should know and respect what a child wants to do and learn, the student should know and respect what teachers and parents want children to do and learn. The trick is how over time to reach an accommodation that both sides can live with. That accommodation can never be without its ups and downs; that is a given.

I am not, of course, suggesting that students be subjected to a series of lectures on productive learning, responsibility, and the "psychology of choosing." What I am suggesting is that the early days of the first year of secondary school be devoted to discussions—conversations about the nature of the contract spelling out roles and mutual obligations of students and teachers in carrying out projects, including the predictable problems such untraditional relationships will encounter. There is a difference between lecturing and discussing, between "telling" and flushing out feelings, ideas, and questions, between employing abstractions and generalizations and staying on the level of concrete experience, issues, and examples. I am describing a "tooling up" process, one in which the tools (their nature and connections) should not be left to the imagination. It is and should not be a one-lesson discussion, if only because the contract is no simple affair both for students and teachers who are forging a relationship new to them. Initially, it will not be easy for them and, therefore, there will be the danger or temptation to fall back into more familiar roles. Productive learning is not smooth sailing.

I spent decades helping graduate students acquire clinical knowledge and skills, diagnostic and therapeutic. It took me several years of bitter experience—as well as a few courageous and forthcoming, assertive students—to realize that I was putting them into situations that were familiar to me but *totally* unfamiliar to them, and that I was insensitive to the feelings, anxieties, and questions plaguing them. Consequently, when I would go over their written or oral reports and point out their many errors of omission and commission, it may have elevated my self-esteem and sense of security but not theirs. In brief, I learned the hard way that I was not starting with where the students were, but telling them what was expected of them as if those expectations would be no source of problem to them. The fact is that I expected them to be and feel incompetent, to make errors that were quite predictable, to come to have doubts about their choice of career, but I most inadequately discussed the whys and wherefores of those reactions with them. It made life difficult for them. I began to prepare them very differently, more interpersonally, and with much more attention to our different starting points. Needless to say, there is no way you can prepare students for an unfamiliar task that inoculates them *and* you against mistakes, misinterpretations, and faulty conclusions.

But, it could be argued, those were graduate students who are a good deal older than those who enter a secondary school. Graduate students have already chosen a career path, the much younger student has not been in the situation where he or she has had to make choices in a context very different from the usual classroom and may require the student to spend time away from that classroom and even the school. Is it not unreasonable to expect these youngsters to understand, even dimly, what they are getting into? You will not be offering them courses like math, science, history, and the like but a menu of projects from which they will have to choose two or three and that will engage them for weeks and perhaps months? Is that a healthy menu for such youngsters? There are several answers. The first is that many of these youngsters will have already carried out a project of sorts dear to their hearts and into which they poured a great deal of time and energy often mystifying to parents. Hobbies are projects that can vary from the simple and nonchallenging to what is complex in its problem-solving aspects. It is an egregious error to restrict the concept of education to that which takes place in the encapsulated classroom in the encapsulated school. It is the case, unfortunately, that the educational literature says little about what children do and learn and *why* outside of school that enlarges their knowledge and increases their motivation to learn. We may call it informal learning but that does not mean that it lacks many of the ingredients and consequences of learning in school. Not infrequently, the informal is more productive than the formal in terms of self-directedness, sustained motivation, and lasting effects. The second answer, related to the first, is that these students know full well the difference between sitting and learning and doing and learning, just as they know the difference between wanting and having to learn, as well as the difference between the sense of growth and the feeling that they are ritualistically going through the motions in order to satisfy an adult's purposes. The third answer is that what I am proposing has been done many times in many schools, albeit as a very small part of the school experience. What I am proposing would take up most of a student's school experience, if not all of it. The final answer is that as educators our obligation is not to teach but to challenge, to capitalize on students' interests and not to ignore them, to eschew the imagery of the empty vessel *we* must fill, and to give up the myth that it is only when we fill the vessel to the brim will students be capable of making choices and taking responsibility for those choices. Intellectual growth, like physical growth, is a continuous process dependent on "inside and outside" factors. The vessel gets filled as much (if not more) by what goes on in and comes from the inside than from the outside, and if we ignore or downplay that inside world we may end up with a filled vessel at the end of formal schooling—the tests have been passed, the diploma has been awarded—except that the student is relieved that his or her years of imprisonment are over and maybe *now* their individuality stands a chance of being recognized and exploited. For many students the expectation will never be realized. Indeed, many students want nothing more to do with school; psychologically, they dropped out before they were graduated. I need say nothing of that large number who did drop out.

Let us turn to the menu of projects. Here are a few examples of topics:

1. The features of town or city government, with special emphasis on one of its departments and services.
2. The location and functions of senior citizen centers, i.e., who goes there and when.
3. How is air or water pollution detected and prevented?
4. What are functions of banks, i.e., their services, sources of income, etc.?
5. Why do local governments have budgets? What are their sources of income? How is the tax rate computed and who decides rates?
6. What does an annual physical exam consist of and why?
7. How do life insurance companies determine the costs of policies?
8. What is a nonprofit agency? How many are in the town or city? How do they sustain their existence?
9. What is a political party? How do you join one? How does it function?
10. How has the town, city, or neighborhood changed and why?
11. When, how, and why did the families of your parents come to this country?
12. How many musical or drama groups are there in the community? Who are their members? Where and when do they perform and how often?

13. What is involved in taking and analyzing a poll of opinion about people's attitudes, interests, and choices?
14. Where does the drinking water for the community come from, how is it made safe for human use, and what kind of knowledge and training do those responsible for the water system have?

I can assure the reader that the list can go on and on, its length a function of many factors of which imagination and knowledge of a community's ordinariness and distinctiveness are but two of the factors. The few examples I have given are those that are or can be made relevant to traditional subject matter: history, social studies, chemistry, science, and math.[2] Each of them requires the students to be out of the classroom for a significant period of time. Needless to say, many of these examples could be developed into a doctoral dissertation. Let me hasten to point out that many graduate students come up with proposals that fail to distinguish between a career and a thesis. It is the obligation of the teacher—the secondary school teacher and the dissertation advisor—to help frame the project so that it is both doable in a given period of time and is compatible with the student's capabilities and available resources. The teacher is an available advisor, coach, and multifaceted resource. In the case of secondary school teachers there is an additional task and that is to be sensitive as to when the student (or small group of students) could benefit from formal instruction in relevant subject matter. That, in my experience, is frequently the case with the graduate student in regard to problems of method, theory, and the work of others. Similarly, just as the doctoral student has a dissertation committee, so may the secondary school student have a committee.

It is beyond my purpose to present a detailed plan for the organization of the secondary school. That would require a book in itself. My sole purpose has been to suggest how, taking contexts of productive learning seriously, there are alternative ways of thinking about and organizing these schools, and that these ways radically transform the nature of and the relations between student and teacher, as well as between both of them and the community, and, finally, between self-directed action and experience, on the one hand, and the acquisition of organized subject matter, on the other hand.

I have no doubt that the school I am describing will strike readers as messy. We are so used to the factory-like organization of the school that my proposal will seem to be describing and advocating chaos, anarchy, or both. *The hallmark of imprisonment in a long-standing tradition is the inability or unwillingness to consider any truly significant alteration in that tradition, especially if it will require you to think and act in unfamiliar ways. That is not in principle an undesirable reaction. Tradition should not lightly, let alone unre-*

flectively, be changed. But, when in the case of schools that tradition is failing in its purposes and achievements, when efforts to change that tradition have been discernibly unproductive of improvement, when that intractability is puzzling practically to everyone and is seen as a source of and not an antidote to major social problems—when that tradition has these features, the days of tinkering or passive resignation to the status quo should be considered over.

For my purpose my proposal is one way of indicating how contexts of productive learning can be a basis for organizing secondary schools. Others may come up with a different plan, but it is inconceivable to me that any plan that takes productive learning seriously, that is explicitly a reaction to and recognition of the failures of these schools as they are, will not require sharp breaks with the tradition. And neither my plan nor those of others will be free of myriad problems, both predictable and unpredictable.

My suggestions are in no danger of being taken seriously, let alone implemented. I would not deny the validity of the criticism that I really have not come up with what could be called a plan. What I have done is presented a rationale by which any plan should be judged. What national discussion on school reform calls for is far less a plan than an examination of the differences between contexts of productive and unproductive learning and what organizational transformations those differences may and will require, which is to say that the national discussion could clarify the nature and implications of those differences. Today we do not need detailed plans but rather an increased awareness that those differences are sufficiently stark so as to require us to take productive learning more seriously than ever before. Without understanding those differences we will never be able to make a commitment to undertake the transformation of schools. Understanding and commitment are the first steps without which we will continue to demonstrate that the more things change the more they remain the same.[3]

What does all of this have to do with governance? The overall answer is that what I am proposing will never get a hearing by or get off the ground from forces within the system. What the system can do and has done is: Repair this, repair that, but leave the system intact! Except for one feature the governance of the school will be the same as I described for elementary school, i.e., teachers and parents will be the governors. In some respects the parental role will be even more crucial because the relationships between school and community will be far more frequent and intimate than in the case of the elementary school. As people who live and work in the community, parents are not without knowledge and connections relevant to topics and sites for projects. And precisely because students will not be spending all their time each day and month of the school year in a classroom, the cooperation and commitment of parents are morally and educationally essential. Whatever arguments I advanced for parent–teacher governance of elementary schools are no less applicable to secondary schools. The only feature I would add is that the governing group have on it two or three members of the community (who may or may not be parents) who are willing to serve because they are sympathetic to the endeavor, and who by virtue of experience, status, and accomplishments can be very helpful in opening up doors in the community for students and teachers. If anything is clear in my proposal it is that the boundaries between school and community will be very porous, i.e., throughout the secondary school years students will be spending more and more investigative time outside of school than informal instruction in school.

In 1983 I wrote *Schooling in America: Scapegoat and Salvation.* The book went out of print very silently and quickly. It was what is called a "critical success": The reviewers applauded it but for all practical purposes no one read it. The book was about the difference between productive and unproductive contexts of learning. In that book I discuss a program designed to improve science education in the middle schools, and I did so less because it is typical and more because it has been described and evaluated in an atypically comprehensive and judicious way. It is quite instructive in regard to what I have said about schools and community resources.

I refer to Project City Science, a program carried out by New York University in conjunction with several junior high schools in poor New York neighborhoods. Funding came from the National Science Foundation. The purpose of the project was "to help bring about a major, lasting and self-perpetuating improvement, principally in New York City, in the teaching of science in the middle grades between elementary and high school" (Longo, 1979, p. 12). Longo went on to state:

> While the rationale for placing primary emphasis on science rather than on other subjects, such as reading and mathematics, is not clearly stated, it is evident that the proposers of [Project City Science] PCS feel that science is an area in which instruction is particularly ineffective. It is noted that:
>
>> science teaching at the middle school level in New York City and many other cities can only be regarded, on the whole, as gravely inadequate ... [Furthermore,] science education in the city elementary schools remains woefully weak, when not absent altogether.

Having concluded that, "improving elementary school science in the cities seems to be an intractable problem of massive proportions," project staff apparently decided that the middle school (i.e., grades 6–9) should become the logical focus of their efforts. The reasons offered for this appear to be threefold. First, a large fraction of inner city youth do not go on to attend high school, and so efforts made at a later stage would be too late. Second, by the time students reach high school, a deep antipathy toward the study of science has already developed, and so they will usually not choose to take courses in science. Third, even though many educators agree that the junior high school years may be critical for students, very little emphasis has been placed on developing procedures that improve instruction or modernize curriculum at this level—particularly in science.

The proposal goes on to clearly emphasize its junior high school focus. For many city youngsters, junior high school provides the *only* formal instruction in science they receive in their lives! ... it constitutes quantitatively the most science they will formally encounter.

Project emphasis was not solely on the direct improvement of science instruction in the school, but on the development of a model program for training junior high school science teachers as well. The intent was both to provide science teachers for the New York City middle schools, and to develop a training model with widespread potential. The then Project Director, interviewed for an article about PCS, indicated what the program's major concerns were:

> First, we're doing inservice training of teachers who are already in the schools. Second, we're designing a training program for the whole next generation of junior high school teachers. Third, we're working to analyze instructional problems and devise system-wide solutions.... Over the long run, [the director] can envision Project City Science helping to effect a new kind of science teaching.... If Project City Science succeeds, and if it is duplicated in other cities, in ten years we could replace up to 40 percent with a cadre of science teachers trained for the job.... What we want to develop is a design that can be used in city schools throughout the country, something that can be adopted quickly by other universities and other school districts. (pp. 12–13)

One more quotation is relevant to the major problems the project was created to address:

> Assuming, then, that there is an especially urgent need to improve science instruction during the transition years, what are the particular problems that must be solved or at least ameliorated? The 1974 proposal explicitly claimed, and Project experience has subsequently supported, that *three major problems exist:*
>
> 1. *The failure of teacher training,* both preservice, and inservice, to prepare science teachers to deal effectively with the early adolescent child in the inner-city situation.
> 2. A continuous reliance on *science programs that do not reflect* sufficiently what has been learned in the last decade or so about science curricula and new approaches to teaching science.

3. *A scarcity of systematic* knowledge about the age group and about what conditions and techniques best promote an *interest in a learning of science* at that age and in inner-city circumstances.

Implicit in the proposal and accentuated by Project experience is a fourth problem: *The failure* on all sides to identify, organize, and bring to *bear in a coordinated way* the not inconsiderable *material and human resources* of the state, city, district schools, universities, and community at large. Related to this is the problem of establishing a self-sustaining system for continuing reform rather than merely instituting this or that improvement, regardless of how alluring a given reform seems to be in the short run, or however much desired by one or the other agency or institution. (Longo, 1979, p. 14)

The problems were many but it was recognized that among the most crucial was how to engender in pupils an interest in science. More correctly, how first to overcome *antipathy* and then to engender and sustain interest.

I have gone into detail about this project to make a point that, once made, will seem obvious. Indeed, the point is so obvious that it apparently required no statement or examination by the creators of the project or, for that matter, by the people at the National Science Foundation who decided to fund this and similar efforts. (Let us not scapegoat the project directors. We can assume that the project was scrutinized by a variety of specialists for whom the obvious also was literally unremarkable.) *Insofar as the schools were concerned, the emphasis was almost exclusively on the classroom—that was where interest was to be engendered and productive learning to take place. It was in the classroom that success would be judged by changes in test scores over time. For all practical purposes, learning and experiencing science outside school—utilizing "the not inconsiderable material and human resources of the state, city, district schools, universities, and community at large"—were not in the picture.* We can assume that Project City Science did engender more interest in students, but there is nothing in the evaluation to suggest that it was other than a sometime thing. Experience since that project does not permit a favorable judgment.

Let us turn to an interview printed in the *New York Times* on April 6, 1982. Again it is about the appalling quality of science education in New York city schools, this time more than a decade after Longo's evaluation of Project City Science. The interview was with the dean for science in the College of Liberal Arts and Science of the City University of New York.

Dean Harry Lustig described the severity of the shortage of math and science teachers: In the previous year Connecticut had graduated *no one* certified to teach high school science; Minnesota had graduated one person; in Chicago there was only one licensed physics teacher for every two high schools;

throughout the country 22% of high school mathematics teaching posts were vacant and 26% of posts were filled either by non-certified or by temporarily certified teachers. Lustig offered two reasons for this serious shortage. First, anyone with a science or mathematics background can make more money in industry than in teaching. Second:

> If you haven't been motivated, haven't had the foundation for science in junior high school, it may very well be too late. Let's face it, the sciences are hard and we're living in a very soft world. Students are allowed to take electives instead of hard courses. We've had a fantastic decrease in the number of students signing up for the hard sciences. They'd rather take easy subjects and get higher grades.

I sympathize with the dean's concerns but not with his diagnosis. He was seeing the problem from the perspective of the subject matter of science as if that subject existed outside time and history. The fact is that in the past there was both no shortage of science and math teachers (in fact, there was an oversupply) *and* no evidence that the quality of teaching was better or that students found these courses more interesting than they do today. Indeed, the orbiting by Russia of the first sputnik in 1957 catalyzed a national uproar about the outmoded and stultifying math and science curricula to which students were exposed. It may well be that in past decades math and science teachers "knew" their subject matter far better than teachers today but there is no reason to believe that this knowledge made science more interesting for students.

During the decade of the fifties I spent a good deal of time in junior high and high schools, and one had to be especially dense not to be aware of the plight of science teachers and their students. I take no satisfaction in having predicted that the new math and science curricula that began to be introduced in the late fifties and early sixties would confirm the maxim that the more things change the more they remain the same. That prediction may have been wrong: The situation has not remained the same, it has gotten worse. Here, again, we see the fallacy that knowledge of subject matter— knowledge independent of how the structure and skills of that subject matter arose from transactions between thinking and action, between the reciprocal influences of the internal processes of investigators and external phenomena—can be assimilated in a meaningful way by passive students in a classroom. (Parenthetically, in the interview Lustig expresses the opinion that the teaching of science in private schools is as poor and motivation extinguishing as it is in public schools.)

Let me now present the major reason I find the interview significant. Asked about the possibility of colleges dealing directly with students in secondary schools, Lustig replied:

We've had pilot programs like this and they have worked very well at City College. In cooperation with the New York Academy of Science we have a summer research program for junior high school students.

They come in very scared. These are all minority kids from the South Bronx and they are on grade level, but they are not selected for being particularly outstanding in science. We put them into research labs and they really learn something about science. They change, many of them completely—they become confident of themselves in science.

How do we account for these results, which are by no means unusual, as anecdote on anecdote would attest? The fact that these junior high school students had a sustained experience outside school is not in itself educationally significant. What is significant are two features of the experience: They could observe adults *working* at science, and, we can assume, they participated in activities that at their level were in principle similar to those in which their mentors were engaged. For these junior high school students, science was not an abstraction or a set of principles, laws, and procedures to be learned by rote or in a sociophysical context in which what one does seems to be unconnected to the real world and to be important only in terms of a grade.

It apparently could not occur to the dean that not only could the summer experiences of these junior high students not be replicated in the school but that perhaps they should not be replicated. Project City Science had emphasized New York City's near limitless resources *potentially* for educational purposes. What the dean reported was but one way in which community resources can be exploited by schools. New York City is, as it usually is, atypical in its resources. But it is not atypical in the way in which the school system keeps the community and its resources at a distance. The governance system of our schools insures that education will be defined only in terms of what students and teachers do in encapsulated classrooms in encapsulated schools.

The existence of schools as bounded, isolated entities is the single most effective barrier to wedding subject matter and experience in ways that are sustaining, enlivening, and broadening. The fact that schools exist as they do has the effect of separating rather than integrating subject matter and active experience, of separating the concrete from the abstract, of perpetuating the enormous gulf between received and experienced knowledge. I said earlier that in the post–World War II era a major industry has grown up centering on the following questions. How do we make schools more interesting places? How can we help students to see that subject matter can be both interesting and important? The diversity of answers has been enormous, and quite costly, but with very few exceptions they assumed that the questions could be successfully answered by *making changes within* the school.[4] As I have emphasized, we have failed to recognize the possibility that the school building is a very large part of the problem and that changes in the world view of post–World War II generations have made the traditional conception of school and schooling more problematic than ever before. Indeed, this era has experienced a nostalgic yearning for that Golden Age in which students did what they were supposed to do, learned what they were supposed to learn, and forever enjoyed the fruits of their schooling; that schools have never been interesting places for the bulk of students has been glossed over with the justification that the end justifies the means, even though the ends are vaguely defined (if they are defined at all). When I discussed my proposal for governance of the elementary school, I attempted to deal with what I thought would be the major criticisms of or reservations about the proposal. There is no need for me to repeat that discussion here. What I do feel is necessary here is that I state in skeleton form the steps that led to my proposal.

1. The differences, and their consequences, between productive and unproductive contexts of learning were made clear long before I was born. In that regard, I bring nothing new to the table.
2. It has long been the case that classrooms are places where violations of contexts of productive learning are by far the rule and not the exception.
3. The governance system of schools—its history, form, and development—has never been geared to recognize and respect individuality and to create and sustain contexts of productive learning.
4. The governance system involves far more than a single school or school system. It also includes a state department of education, legislative and executive branches of government (local, state, and federal), colleges and universities, and parents. If these stakeholders are part of the system, it is also the case that they are either uncoordinated parts, or in conflict with each other, or for all practical purposes unknown to each other.
5. That kind of system insures that: (a) Much that goes on in a single classroom or school is determined by the policies and decisions of others with no knowledge of the classroom and school; (b) departures from the ethos and dictates of the system are extraordinarily difficult and more often than not impossible; (c) system-correcting processes are notable by their absence; and (d) accountability is, to say the least, diffuse, puzzling, if not downright mysterious.
6. There is no agreement within the system about an overarching purpose of schooling. There are many purposes each of which has call on time, money, and resources, and this is a consequence of the different agendas and power of different parts of the system.

7. In the post–World War II era efforts to change or reform the system, let alone improve educational outcomes, have failed. There are isolated instances (and they are isolated) where the rationale for productive learning has been taken seriously with varying degrees of success, but the evidence is overwhelming that the system is not geared to *sustain* these efforts or to seek to *spread* them to other parts of the system. It is not a system that "learns." It is not a system geared to exploit singularities but one to maintain uniformity.

8. There are two stakeholders who are physically and psychologically related to schools as no other stakeholders. They (and students) are directly affected by policies and decisions made by others in the system. The two stakeholders are teachers and parents, and my proposal gives them the responsibility to govern the school: to formulate policies, develop budgets, select personnel, and with resources to purchase support services necessary to carry out policies and decisions. These are support services that are in no way related to or controlling of policies and decisions.

9. The political principle is that those who are affected by decisions should stand in a meaningful relation to those decisions and in the case of schools that means that parents and teachers should be the governors. *Unless those stakeholders understand and are committed to an overarching purpose centering on contexts of productive learning, the spirit of the political principle may be manifest but little or nothing else will change.*

10. My proposal requires legislation that would encourage and support the parents and teachers of any school to take full responsibility for that school if they can make a convincing case that they understand and are committed to create and sustain contexts of productive learning to the extent that their stated plan clearly is a departure from schools as we know them. The legislation is permissive, not directive.

11. There is no way that the spirit and goal of *any* proposal to take seriously the differences between productive and unproductive learning can be implemented without realistically assuming that the initial plan is just that: an initial plan (Model A) that should be improved and superseded by a second plan (Model B). The educational reform literature is replete with examples of reform efforts that had not built into them self-correcting or self-improving forums and processes justifying an improved model.

12. My proposal does take us on uncharted seas. If that is not (as it is not) inherently virtuous, neither is it inherently unworthy or unworkable. If the present governance system is allowed to continue there will be many changes in teacher morale, student behavior and achievements,

parental resentment, public hostility, "do something, do anything" policies, and a continued slow disintegration of the public and school system. None of these changes is new. There is literally no good reason
why these changes should stop. We have had a surfeit of rhetoric and
cosmetics.

Any system of governance, whether it be in education, politics, business, or a church rest on conceptions of what people are, what they can be,
what they need, and what the system owes them. In the political sphere that
conception is contained in our constitution and the amendments to it. Those
amendments are crucially instructive because each was a deliberate departure from previous thought and practice, not a cosmetic or token gesture,
and the consequences of each was impossible to predict with security, let alone
certainty. Each amendment in some very important way changed the game
and the score, i.e., the system. In each case the amendment was powered by,
among other things, moral considerations people no longer could ignore. And
in the case of most amendments (probably all, I am no historian) there were
opponents who viewed the amendments as instances where the cure was worse
than the disease, where dramatically altering some important part of the system was subversive of long-standing tradition. Giving the vote to women,
for example—not some far off day but now—was perceived in many quarters as based on a faulty psychology, a misreading of history, a misunderstanding of the practical realities of this world, and an inexcusable indulgence
of the worst features of utopian thinking. (Women, like students in our schools
and parents and teachers in my proposal, were seen as having more deficits
than assets and, therefore, unable to assume a significant degree of responsibility.) The amendments were made possible because the people or representatives in at least two-thirds of the states approved them. The system did
not change because of external pressures but internal ones. That has not
been the case in educational governance.

In the past century, and after compulsory universal education was
achieved, there have been only two instances when the system changed in
an important respect. Both had their source outside the system. The first
was the 1954 desegregation decision, and the second was the 1975 "main-
streaming" legislation. In both instances schools were forced to do what they
had previously not done but could have done. Outside of the South most
people (and more than a few in the South) knew in their heart of hearts
that blacks were, educationally speaking, second-class citizens, and many people breathed a sigh of relief that the court had ruled as it did. And it was
similarly so in the case of handicapped children, some of whom had not
been allowed in school and those who were had been segregated. Indeed,
the legislation was, legally speaking, a direct consequence of the court's

decision. Having lived through the period when the decision and legislation took place and the process of implementation begun, it was my distinct impression that the major governors of the school system were totally unprepared in regard to administering the new state of affairs. And that is the point: It was seen as an administrative problem, not a governance one. Should the governance system change in any way? Should that system develop forums and processes that would allow it to be more sensitive and responsive (and quickly) to problems that would arise? Should more authority and responsibility be given to those educational personnel and parents who were closest to the children and the classroom? Should the process for selection of those who will govern be altered so as to give formal representation to those who previously were "out of the loop"? Could those who governed continue to assume that schools could and should remain isolated oases in communities where conflict and passion would be both predictable and strong? By interpreting what they faced as a problem of administration and management, the governance system remained intact, a stance that subsequent years proved to be shortsighted in the extreme. A governance system that is layered and whose parts are blatantly uncoordinated will produce policies unrelated to the contexts they seek to affect (Pauly, 1991).

I hold out no hope that the present governance system can create and sustain contexts of productive learning. That is why my proposals have to assume the passage of legislation that would encourage and support parents and teachers of a school to assume the task of creating, sustaining, and overseeing that school in the most explicit and concrete ways so that it will be unlike schools they have known. That school will not be part of a current system but very much related to other schools that take advantage of the opportunity the legislation provides. Are there guarantees in moving in these ways? No. Will there be problems, potholes, and mistakes? Yes. Is the current governance system adequate to the problems it faces? No. Is there very good evidence that the governance system is a large part of the problem and cannot be part of the solution? Yes. Is there evidence that the system is rescuable? No. Can we afford—do we have the time—to continue as we have? No. Have you read the 1996 "summit statement" issued by corporate leaders and state governors containing their prescription for school improvement (Sarason & Lorentz, 1997)? Their statement is the oversimplification of the century and an example of "deep down it is shallow." But that conference was preceded by a national publicity campaign and will be followed by action. Their plan is an oversimplification, a reprise of past statements, but you must give them credit for recognizing that the situation cannot, must not, be allowed to continue. And what does the educational community suggest? Do they have a plan? Is it clear what that community stands for? The silence is near total and eerie.

NOTES

[1]I recently received a very personal letter from one of the most responsible educational reformers in the post–World War II era. His efforts changed the nature of the conversation in the field. He was (is) unaware that I was writing this book. I feel it is ethically appropriate to give four sentences from the letter because I have heard identical thoughts in conversation with many other reformers. "You and I both know that they [obstacles to reform] are embedded in the system." "The problem remains, however, why it has to be so difficult. As I listen to superintendents these days, I hear the same honest wailing about the gridlock that characterizes most systems. Add to that the disinterest and utter wrong-headedness of much of the policy discussion, and it nearly drives one hopelessly to drink." Every reformer ends up with increased respect for the ability of the system to maintain the status quo. Educators and schools are infinitely more shaped by the system than they can ever shape the system.

[2]I not only approve acquiring traditional subject matter, but I revere that process. The goal of my proposal is to acquire subject matter in a way that increases the motivation to seek to learn more about subject matter. I take it for granted that if my proposal was taken seriously, all students would have experienced all of subject matter in graded steps by the end of schooling, i.e., by graduation a student will have done several projects in each of the subjects. The number of such projects and their integration with formal instruction I cannot specify. The reader should bear in mind that the type of project I suggest has been done by hundreds (perhaps thousands) of middle and high school students on a one-shot basis. This despite the fact that the preparatory programs of the teachers of these students taught them nothing, or next to nothing, about the potentialities of an enlarged role for such projects, i.e., for all practical purposes the preparatory programs rivet on and do not go beyond what can be done in the encapsulated classroom.

[3]For example, education in the arts is viewed as a frill, not as a subject matter that in the past and the present has been related to and illuminating of history, mathematics, science, literature, and social studies. Nor is artistic activity conceived, as it should be, as one willingly engaged in by preschoolers, an activity rather thoroughly extinguished in school. I refer the reader to my book, *The Challenge of Art to Psychology* (1990b) and to John Dewey's classic, *Art as Experience* (1934). From the standpoint of career opportunities in the arts I urge the reader to reflect on Herbert's op-ed column in the *New York Times,* Friday, June 7, 1996. Art education is the first victim of budget reduction. As Herbert says, "It is not possible to overstate the importance of legitimate career opportunities of the legion of kids who come out of New York's public schools each year. That the schools themselves would slam the door on some of those opportunities is incomprehensible." It is not incomprehensible. Respect for individuality and contexts for productive learning is not the purpose of schools—it is as comprehensible and dispiriting as that.

[4]In 1996 The Center for Instructional Research and Curriculum Evaluation (CIRCE) at the University of Illinois published *Strategies: Teacher Professional Development in Chicago School Reform.* It is well worth reading, especially because of the final chapter by Robert Stake, Director of CIRCE. With refreshing candor and concreteness, Dr. Stake makes it clear that the *minimal* conditions for achieving any-

thing resembling a modest, non-cosmetic change—about anything, *I* conclude—do not exist. Chicago is not atypical. Dr. Stake's chapter deserves wide circulation. Just as he knows the difference between evidence and opinion, he knows the difference between a problem-producing and problem-sustaining system, on the one hand, and one that takes seriously its rhetoric, on the other hand. (The publication can be obtained from CIRCE.)

The Preparation of Educators

In an earlier chapter I stressed that when we used the words *educational system* we should mean more than a single school system. What goes on in a single school system is incomprehensible apart from the role of other stakeholders. One of those stakeholders, the focus of this chapter, are colleges and universities. In a legal–formal sense colleges and universities do not govern schools, but because of their role in selecting, preparing, and informally credentialing educators, they impact on schools, they interact and depend on each other. The relationship is not without tension, problems, and conflict. Privately, school personnel do not, generally speaking, admire how colleges carry out their mission. Again, privately, college faculty do not have admiration for what schools are and for the quality of educational outcomes. College faculty judge themselves as superior to school personnel in regard to scope of knowledge about research and theory as well as about the history and foundations of the educational enterprise. School personnel see college faculty as semi-lost in the clouds of theory and unknowledgeable about and/or insensitive to the realities schools face today. It is a relationship of interdependence. Neither could exist without the other. But existing as each does in different institutional cultures and history, the relationship has many problematic aspects (Sarason, 1992). Rhetoric aside, the two parts are by no means in agreement about the overarching purpose of schooling. Indeed, they never even discuss the issue and what that issue requires of each alone and in combination. The result is that each part goes its own way, often at cross purposes or, more frequently, unreinforcing of each other's purpose. This is what I meant when I said that the educational system in its larger sense is an uncoordinated one for which there is no overall, meaningful governance with the responsibility of defining purpose and devoted solely to support the creation and sustaining of contexts of productive learning. I am not advocating that such a governing body is necessary or even practical or desirable. I am not prepared to make such a judgment. The point I am making is in the nature of a fact: The educational system is uncoordinated in at least two major respects. The first is that the stakeholders or parts of the system are, at best, uncoordinated and, at worst, contributors to each other's inadequacies, failures, and resistance to change. The second, discussed in earlier chapters, is that in what is conventionally called a school system, incoordination of parts is the rule, not the exception. Incoordination in a system is the hallmark of the unwillingness or inability of parts to agree on purpose, process, and means for self-correction. A governance system not powered by and committed to an overarching purpose inevitably shows all the features of incoordination and a drop in the quality of whatever the system is supposed to "produce." That is an obvious fact in the private sector, and it is no less obvious in educational systems, albeit many people either cannot see or take the obvious seriously.

What follows in this chapter rests on observations I really regard as established facts:

1. School personnel do not value highly what they were exposed to and experienced in preparatory programs.
2. Within the educational community and beyond (well beyond) there has been increasing recognition that improving the quality of educational personnel and practice requires changes *both* in schools *and* colleges. (It is assumed that that can be achieved in the current system. In light of what I have said previously about the culture, style, and governance of these two stakeholders, I regard that assumption as unwarranted and amazingly optimistic because, as I shall soon indicate, neither of these parts have governance systems supportive of other than cosmetic change, i.e., neither has a track record for departures from tradition, to understate the point.)

Let us begin with a proposal made by Dr. Kenneth Wilson whose 1996 book *Redesigning Education* I regard as a seminal work and who in a 1994 paper presented a proposal for the development of teachers. I start with that proposal because it is so beautifully illustrative of what I endeavored to suggest about schools committed to creating and sustaining contexts of productive learning. His proposal is preceded by an imaginary anecdote that I shall paraphrase in my own words. "Imagine that at age 20 or so I come to the conclusion that I want to be a violinist. So I go to the Julliard School of Music, and I ask to become a student there. They will look at me with staring disbelief and then inform me that they only consider students who can demonstrate that they have a facility with and an aptitude for the violin. They never would consider a student whose experience with the violin was zero and who clearly has no understanding of the time, energy, and commitment required to become only proficient with the instrument. Even if I came and could demonstrate that I was already proficient, that would not be sufficient. They seek to select individuals who demonstrate more than technical proficiency. Being able to read notes and give auditory expression to them are not enough. If after they turned me down I decided that I would become a teacher, I would have little or no trouble getting into a program even though I never taught anything to anybody. Unless my appearance and behavior were in some ways aberrant, I was in. In a 1- or 2-year program, most of which will be spent in courses, I will be entitled to teach, to be an independent practitioner." It is no wonder that in the past two decades the professional development of teachers has occupied the attention of a number of respected individuals, e.g., Linda Darling Hammond and Anne Lieberman. And when these educators discuss professional development they mean more, much more, than taking more courses.[1]

Wilson's proposal concerns action *antedating* entrance into a preparatory program. His proposal is that *beginning in fifth or sixth grade all students should experience the role of a teacher and that such experience should be continued throughout the school years*. He gives several major arguments for the proposal.

1. That kind of hands-on experience is necessary for anyone who may at a later point consider teaching as a career, and it would provide the preparatory program a source of data for deciding whether teaching is or is not appropriate for candidates. It would also be both a spur and a basis for such programs to use their resources in ways more growth stimulating and more intellectually–conceptually broad than they are now.

2. The experience would provide the student knowledge of the factors involved when one works and cooperates with another individual in

an intimate, interpersonal relationship, i.e., the kind of relationship in which in later "real" life the student will find him- or herself in work or as a parent or in any instance in which one person seeks in some way to influence and/or help someone else. What one person owes another person, what facilitates learning, what impedes learning, the complexities of teaching and learning—these are understandings indicative of the understandings one would want the student to grasp *over time.*

3. When students are seen as assets which can be exploited for the personal and intellectual benefit for them and others, they can become a resource that in economic terms contributes to an increase in productivity: Educational outcomes are increased both in quantity and quality without corresponding increase in costs.

That students, even as early as those in the fifth or sixth grades, can be in a one-on-one teaching role will not come as news to some school personnel. And if teachers in the legendary one-room schoolhouse could respond to the proposal, they too would not consider it news. That does not mean that in the long past and today the potentialities of this student role were and are being exploited. So, for example, I know of no instance where that role has been institutionalized and informed by the spirit and goals of Wilson's proposal. We are at the point where we do not have a Model A in place and in ways that provide a basis for developing Model B, and so on.

Every argument against my governance proposals that I took up in earlier chapters will be employed by some people against Wilson's proposals. My answers here would be the same. Here I wish to comment again on one such argument: "For teachers to do what you are now asking they do is to place an additional burden on them which will take *time,* the most precious commodity in a teacher's working day. If they accepted that task, it would inevitably reduce the time required for achieving the mandated subject matter curriculum." My answer is in several parts. The first is that the proposal puts center stage something that is of enormous significance and interest to students: the nature of learning in its social–personal contexts. Second, the student would learn how and why productive learning requires respect for the individuality of teacher and student, that learning is no routine, impersonal affair. Third, teaching any aspect of any subject matter can be a stimulus to acknowledging that there are other aspects of the subject matter that he or she should or may want to learn, i.e., the more you know the more you need to know. Fourth, over the school years the student can acquire knowledge, a sense of personal competence, and experience a sense of growth rare in the experience of students and so applicable over the lifetime.

The fifth part of my answer concedes the validity of the critic's concern about time: *Given the ways classrooms and schools are organized, and the governance system that directs and controls that organization, that system is incapable of accepting and implementing the proposal.* The rationale for the governance system I proposed is in all respects hospitable to the spirit of Wilson's proposal. The current governance system is allergic not only to proposals that require a dramatic alteration of the way things are, especially if the proposal seems "messy" and does not carry with it a guarantee that it will not require a self-correcting stance and process that substitutes Model B for Model A, and Model C for Model B. That is to say, the proposal has to be able to show near-term benefits, i.e., the quick-fix requirement. Many spokespeople in the educational community complain that they are unfairly pressured to fix things quickly. There is some truth to the complaint, but it is also true that these spokespeople have done a scandalously inadequate job of explaining why the quick fix is literally impossible, and that inadequacy derives in large measure from the fact that the alternatives they offer do not explain the sources of past failures, the proposals they offer are reruns of past failures, and what they offer leaves the present system intact, thus contributing to the feeling widespread among the general public that whatever is rotten in Denmark is far more fundamental than these spokespeople are saying. That widespread feeling is hard for people to articulate but their disappointment and disillusionment are real. No one is telling them what they need to know that would provide them with a basis for asking what the constitutional convention of 1787 asked: Do we try to repair the dangerously inadequate Articles of Confederation or should we start from scratch?

Imagine that Wilson's proposal has been taken seriously and is being implemented. What, we can count on being asked, would that mean for college or university preparatory programs? Who will be selecting students who already have had the teaching experience called for in Wilson's proposal? Why and how might they be required to change? That, in my opinion, is the wrong question. The more appropriate question is: How can schools and college departments of education play a role in implementing and sustaining the purposes of Wilson's proposal? Is the knowledge and experience on which their preparatory programs are based applicable only to much older "students"? Is there anyone who would argue that these programs, concerned as they are with the nature of learning, have nothing to contribute to much younger students who are very far from being sophisticated "teachers" and have had limited but sustained teaching experiences? Are these programs applicable only to young adults in their last 2 years of college or who already have been graduated from college? To so argue is as absurd as to assert that the oxygen atom requires one theory and the hydrogen atom requires a different theory. Don't confuse apples with oranges! What gets overlooked is that apples and oranges are both fruit; they are different and similar.

The point here is one I made in previous chapters. Our educational system has different parts that are very poorly coordinated. Wilson's proposal is directed to what schools should do. Yes, schools should take his proposal seriously but so should our schools of education, if only because they potentially have the knowledge and skills that are required to insure that an innovation in practice is being carried out in ways (the continuous improvement process) that provide a basis for going from Model A to Model B. I have long been resentful of the tendency of reformers and others to direct their blame (and often venom) on schools and their personnel for the plight of our schools. To direct most, and often all, of the blame in that direction is to betray ignorance of the different stakeholders who comprise the system of governance: And one of the most important of those stakeholders are colleges and universities in general and schools of education in particular. The system is so uncoordinated it is no wonder that the general public cannot grasp the nature of that system and why it is one that cannot "learn" from its shortcomings and failures. In my 1992 book *The Case for Change: Rethinking the Preparation of Educators,* I took up aspects of this school–college issue, employing a specific proposal of my own. What follows are excerpts from the chapter in which that proposal is contained and discussed.

What I propose is *not* a course but a year-long field experience for college students that could be called Schools and Society, or the Culture of Schools. Whatever the title, it should in no way suggest that it is a professionally oriented experience. Let me list some of the major experiences to which the undergraduate would be exposed.

1. Students would spend a good deal of time in classrooms at all grade levels, from kindergarten through high schools, including classrooms devoted to handicapped children.
2. During the year they would be apprenticed to or be in a position to observe and talk with principals, school psychologists, school social workers, and other individually oriented clinicians. To whatever extent feasible they would attend faculty meetings as well as those involving school personnel with parents and other community people.
3. They would spend time with the superintendent and his staff, and they would be required to attend board of education meetings. Not only would they attend those meetings but they would have the opportunity to get to know the members so as to become knowledgeable about their background and educational perspectives.

4. Students would be expected to attend all meetings of local officialdom at which educational matters (e.g., school budget) will be discussed and acted on.
5. If the school system has contractual relationships with teachers' and
   administrators' unions, it would be arranged for the students to meet
   and get to know their representatives and, again if possible, to observe
   the process whereby collective bargaining positions are formulated,
   and to observe collective bargaining sessions.

You do not just put students in the "field," tell them to observe this or
that type of event, to spend time with this or that type of person, and expect
them to have the conceptual wherewithal to make appropriate sense of their
experiences. That is why the year-long experience would also include seminars by an anthropologist, a psychologist, a sociologist, a political scientist,
an economist, and a historian—each with expertise about education or at
least a developing interest in the field. A major focus of each seminar would
be not only providing and discussing what each of these fields has learned
about education but testing that learning in relation to a particular school
system, community, and state. The major responsibility of these faculty members would be to provide intellectual, substantive direction to what the students observe and do "in the field."

The year-long experience, for which the students will get full college
credit, would be intellectually and personally demanding. To understand
schools from the several perspectives—derived as that understanding would
be from being in "real" schools with all that that subsumes—would be no easy
task. Indeed, some would say that what I have proposed in outline is too tall
an order for 1 year. The merits of that objection, like the merits of my proposal, cannot be judged by any existing experience. The details of my proposal are, at this point, less important than its intellectual–educational goal:
to provide undergraduates with conceptual frameworks and "live" experience for the purpose of enlarging and deepening their knowledge of and outlook on self, schools, and society. There are thorny problems with my proposal,
but before discussing them I want to draw on some personal experiences and
observations that suggest that more than a few students would be eager to
participate in what would be an elective experience.

For the three decades I and my colleagues, at Yale and elsewhere, taught
courses under the rubric of community psychology. As in the proposal I outlined previously, these courses required students to spend a good deal of time
observing *and* participating in the activities of diverse community settings.
Students were not only helped to understand these settings but to carry out
a research project that interested them and could be related to the existing
literature. Before being permitted to enroll in these courses, students were

explicitly told what the time and intellectual demands on them would be. What surprised me was how many students were willing to commit themselves to these demands. I am sure that there is a self-selective factor in who chooses to engage in the experience. But that is precisely the point: We underestimate the number of undergraduates eager for what some of them call a "hands-on" experience that is personally and intellectually stimulating.

During the sixties, of course, there was no problem attracting students. In recent years, we are told, students are more socially apathetic and only a minuscule number are motivated to engage in, to seek to understand, or to change some aspect of the "real world." That judgment is valid, but only if you go by surface appearances. From my discussions with undergraduates, once you go beyond appearances you find concern, bewilderment, anger, and even anxiety about what they see as a crazy, immoral, disorganized, and disorganizing world. They do not want to be intellectually and socially passive. They desire more than facts and knowledge. They want to understand more and feel they can make a difference. They are far from satisfied with the role of the passive, knowledge-accumulating, knowledge-regurgitating student. They would like to experience the "real world" problems and settings in ways that would give them a sense of personal and intellectual growth. But there are few opportunities that would permit them to have such experiences with the stimulation, support, and guidance of committed faculty.

I do not want to exaggerate what is below the surface of what has been called the "me generations." But neither do I want to leave unchallenged the view that undergraduates today are dramatically less concerned with social issues and disinterested in engaging, personally and intellectually, in settings where those issues are manifest. We can, as we usually do, make the mistake we make with public school students: underestimating the nature, sources, and force of a passionate curiosity to understand self, others, and their social world. In our laudable but misdirected effort to hone skills and pour knowledge into students, curiosity becomes the seed beneath the snow awaiting a change in climatic conditions, a change that may or may not come. *Indeed, one of the goals of my proposal is to enable undergraduates to begin to comprehend the difference between passive and active learning, a difference no less relevant for children in a classroom than for college undergraduates.*

Now for the Achilles heel of my proposal. I know of no undergraduate college—or for that matter any comprehensive university—that has the faculty to implement my proposal. Education as a field of intellectual and social inquiry is far from the mainstream of the social sciences. As a field of inquiry, education commands neither respect nor support. During the sixties and seventies I came to know a number of young, brilliant social scientists whose interests and research were in education. Even though their sparkling abilities gained them respect from their colleagues, they did not obtain positions in colleges or universities of the caliber they deserved. Some left their fields.

Educational processes and institutions will not be productively comprehensible unless viewed from the perspectives of the several social sciences. This does not mean, I hasten to add, that at the present time the social sciences are sitting, so to speak, on a gold mine of knowledge directly relevant to matters educational. That is not the case, unfortunately. What is the case is that each of these disciplines has a distinctive perspective and methodologies that, when applied to education, would be as illuminating as when they have been applied to other facets of societal functioning. Sociologists have done some of the most penetrating studies of hospitals. Political scientists have contributed mightily to our understanding of power relationships in governments, national, state, and local. Anthropologists have made us aware not only about the nature and force of culture in diverse societies but of the practical import of that diversity for our foreign policies. Developmental psychologists have shed much light on the course and vicissitudes of personal, cognitive, and social development. And if you regard history, as I do, as a social science, who would deny the significance of what historians have told us about our past and present.

Potentially, the social sciences can make a distinctive contribution to our understanding of schools and school systems that not only express crucial features of our society but impact on our society in intended and unintended, desirable and undesirable, ways. But for that potential to be realized the social sciences would have to focus on educational policies, practices, and institutions, i.e., to begin to look at them, to be in them, to comprehend them with the same searching seriousness with which an anthropologist approaches a foreign culture; a sociologist, a gang, neighborhood, a hospital, a social class grouping; an economist, the stock market, financial institutions, the budget process; a psychologist, observing and studying problem-solving behavior, motivation, and change in children.

What I have just said is not based only on hope and faith. John Dewey was, among other things, a psychologist. Willard Waller wrote his classic book on the sociology of schools in the thirties. In the post–World War II era there have been a dozen or so social scientists (mostly anthropologists, political scientists, sociologists) whose writings have influenced and changed how we think about schools, educational personnel, and educational policy.[2]

So what we do? I have gotten several answers to the question. The first goes like this: "If you are correct about your assessments of the potential of the social sciences, it is clear that it will be years before that potential will be helpful either to our understanding or practice. Given the enormity of the problems we face, we have to act *now*, we cannot sit back and wait." To which

I reply that, of course, we have to act now, but let us admit that in so doing we have no basis whatsoever for believing that our efforts will be more successful than they have been in the past. If we have the moral courage to admit that, should we not also have the moral courage to take the long-term view, to initiate and support efforts that are promising, albeit uncertain about if, when, and how we will be able to pick the fruits of those efforts? Why are you so ready to eschew the long-term view about educational problems at the same time that you would not think of eschewing that view in regard to the study of fatal or debilitating diseases? Yes, we must act now, but let us realize that we are doing it from necessity and social pressure and not from a track record of which anyone is proud.

A second reaction is, on the surface at least, more telling: "If our track record for changing schools is on the dismal side, is that not also true for changing departments in the university? If we know anything about academic departments, it is their bottomless capacity to resist efforts to change their priorities in regard to what they consider important problems. I know you know that in the university the status of the field of education is somewhat below the level of a second-class citizen. What makes you think that you can elevate the status of departments and schools of education *and* get social science departments willingly to give attention to problems in education? How masochistic can you get?"

There are several parts to my reply. The first is an expression of thanks for recognizing what public officialdom and educational reformers (and, therefore, the general public) are unable to face: changing *any* complicated, traditional institution—be it a school, school system, university, church, or a large corporation—is extraordinarily difficult and problematic. And when I say difficult and problematic I refer not only to implementation but also to attaining conceptual clarity about the complexity of the issues you will confront. Failures in implementation are almost always failures of one's guiding conceptualizations and theories.

The second part of my reply to my realistic and pessimistic critic is that she is both right and wrong. Right in the sense that resistance to change will be the order of the day, and wrong in the sense of ignoring the fact that universities have changed when certain conditions obtained: recognition by the public and socially–politically influential groups that a set of interrelated problems is adversely affecting societal stability or health or values; a similar recognition by significant individuals and groups within the university; the willingness of public and private agencies to help fund the changes; and, often overlooked, the perceived leadership of prestigious universities who appear to be accepting of the change. That last point deserves emphasis if only because in the community of universities a very small number play a large role in shaping opinion about a particular change. In earlier days we heard that Macy's does not tell Gimbel's. That has by no means been true among universities.

With regard to education, no one needs to be persuaded that we are dealing with problems we cannot ignore. And few need to be persuaded that we cannot continue doing what we have done, that what we have done simply has been feckless. We have spent billions trying to improve education, but I have heard no one say, as a Vermont senator said about the Vietnam war, that we should declare victory and leave. We should no longer tolerate the present situation where education is, for all practical purposes, unconnected to the social sciences. Someone said that war is too important to be left to the generals. Education is too important to be left to professional educators. Generals *are* important, and professional educators *are* important. But educators, like generals, have to understand that their understandings and proposals for action and practice have to take into account perspectives missing or minimized in their educational background. But this point meets far less resistance from educators than from social scientists. It is not that social scientists resist getting meaningfully involved in educational matters and institutions but rather that they are so disinterested in education. They are content to leave the field to the generals, and then they criticize what they say and do. It is true that because you cannot lay an egg should not prevent you from passing judgment on its edibility. But when, so to speak, the inedibility of eggs threatens the health of the social fabric, passing judgment is not enough. Should we not go beyond judgment and ask: What can, what should, we do?

My undergraduate proposal attempts to address this question. More correctly, it is an attempt to give force to the question. My concern is not only to increase the pool of people who would seek careers in education but to do this in a way that would be personally and intellectually respectable and demanding, and, in addition, would increase the number of social scientists who could use their different perspectives to broaden and deepen their and our understanding of schools and society. At the present time this is a non-issue. Neither from our national leadership, the social sciences, nor from the scores of intellectually pitiful, repair riveted, quick fix, short-term oriented presidential, state, foundation reports is there any sign of recognition that we have truly left education to the generals, that our existing knowledge is fatefully parochial, that truly radical changes are needed in regard to the ways we customarily think about educational practices, organization, and roles, that the long-term view is not an exercise in fantasy.

One criticism of my argument is that I am making the same mistake we make in regard to our schools: If there is a social problem—teenage pregnancy, reckless drivers, use of addictive drugs, smoking—we ask the schools to "solve" the problem. Schools, these critics say, have become human service settings where we are supposed to save souls and, if we have time and energy, to enrich minds. What the "real world" fails to do schools are supposed to remedy.

My critic, however, is quite wrong. True, schools were not conceived as clinical and social service agencies. But the social sciences were conceived as disciplines for the study of people, institutions, and society. The adjective *social* was not chosen at random. And it has not been the case that the social sciences, like the natural sciences, justify their existence only on the basis of contributing to knowledge. Undergirding the social sciences is the belief that enlarging our fund of knowledge contributes, directly or indirectly, to the public welfare. And there is another belief: To contribute to our understanding of people, institutions, and society requires transaction with them. No, the rationale for the social sciences makes inexplicable and inexcusable their disinterest in education, especially today when the inadequacies of our educational system are seen as threatening to our *social* systems.

In taking this stance I do not wish to convey the impression that if the social sciences become more interested in matters educational, the dusk-like quality of our understandings will quickly take on the luster of sunlight. But my respect for the problems social science has illuminated convinces me that over time their contribution to matters educational will be both theoretically and practically significant. Before World War II, anthropology was a very small academic discipline that seemingly had little of practical import for or use by our society. Then came World War II and its immediate aftermath. The United States became a global power responsible administratively for diverse, so-called primitive societies and, in addition, having to deal in all kinds of ways with countries whose cultures we hardly understood. Almost overnight government and other funding sources came to see anthropology as important to our national interests and security. When will we all realize that it is in our national interest to stimulate attention to education in fields that can help alter education in fundamental ways?

Let me return to where we started in this chapter: the relation between primary prevention and my undergraduate proposal. We do not need any more studies to inform us that for most teachers—and I would say for *all* who begin in an urban school—their initial year or so is an unsettling experience during which idealism succumbs to the realities of the school culture. That unsettling, and frequently destabilizing, process has many sources, all of which can be subsumed under "I never really knew that this is the way things would be." These teachers feel alone, bewildered, inadequate, resentful, oscillating between self-blame, castigating the "system," and blaming the irrelevance of much that they had experienced and been told in their preparatory programs. This is not to say that their experience is without any satisfaction or accomplishment or that they are eager to get on the psychoanalytic couch. But they have been shocked by the disjunction between what they are faced with and what they expected to be faced with.

It is not that they were misled but that they were not provided with ways of understanding the culture of classrooms, schools, and school systems. And by understanding I mean possessing conceptualizations, rooted in experience, that sensitize you to what your future experiences will likely be and the ways by which you can cope with predictable problems. The new teacher, for example, is surprised and disappointed by the feeling of aloneness, the lack of collegiality, an unwanted social and intellectual privacy, but he or she has also not been provided with possible ways to cope with, to change, to ameliorate the untoward consequences of such alienation. Indeed, it has not been instilled in teachers that it is their professional and ethical *responsibility* to forge a collegiality productive for their and their students' personal, social, intellectual, development. The preparation of teachers is exclusively concerned with their responsibility to students, not with the responsibility of teachers to themselves and their colleagues. That omission is obviously not helped any by the preparation of educational administrators whose view of collegiality is as superficial as it is self-defeating. *If the collegial conditions do not exist wherein teachers can learn, change, and grow, they cannot create and sustain those conditions for productive learning in their students.*

My undergraduate proposal is not intended to be part of a preparatory program for educators. It is intended to give the students an intensive, demanding experience, e.g., providing perspectives each of which adds to and round out their comprehension of the complexity we call a school system. If we learn how to provide such an experience consistent with its overarching goal, we can help students toward more than a superficial understanding of what I call the culture of schools and school systems. I emphasize *understanding* as an antidote to adherence to misleading stereotypes, to unreflective indulgence of premature judgments, to simplemindedness at the expense of thinking, to a focus on deficits and inadequacies that ignores opportunities and potential assets, to the potent tendency to miss the forest for the trees, to the confusion between what is and what might or should be. Rushing to judgment is easy. Understanding is hard to attain, *especially in regard to a setting that influenced you in diverse ways and toward which you have attitudes you absorbed, not attitudes you thought through.*

I would expect that some, perhaps many, of those who elect to have such an experience will have given some thought to the possibility of a career in education. The experience could provide them with a far more realistic basis for making a career decision than is now the case. They would not later enter a professional program ignorant of schools, uncritically hospitable to whatever they are told, eager more to be trained than to be educated. I have had fairly extensive experience with students in teacher preparation programs. Foremost among the conclusions I came to were, first, how narrow their understanding of the school culture was and, second, how much of their interest and training were in and about the encapsulated classroom. They were almost completely ignorant of how and why schools and school systems are organized and administered as they are; the nature and variety of decision-making processes and forums; the opportunities for and obstacles to change and innovation; the functions, status, and power of specialized nonteaching personnel; and issues of formal and informal power. Stated another way, they are, for all practical purposes, unequipped or not required to think about almost all the factors that will impinge on them, shape them as persons and professionals, determine their self-esteem or personal worth, and stimulate or inhibit their creativity and intellectual growth. My undergraduate proposal is intended to prevent, to some degree, the unfortunate consequences of an uninformed career choice and a stance toward professional preparation that results in tunnel vision.

One might argue that an unintended consequence of my proposal is to discourage people from seeking a career in education by exposing them to the unpleasant realities of what schools are and the seemingly overwhelming problems confronting them. That would happen only if the undergraduate experience concentrated more on inadequacies of schools than on their assets and opportunities, if it focused on what is and not what could be, if it did not provide a vision based on an understanding of institutional and societal change, if that understanding did not provide a basis for realistic courses of action.

Let us take the extreme case where no student decides to seek a career in education. That, from my standpoint, would be disappointing but by no means invalidate the major purposes of the proposal: to provide undergraduates an intellectually respectable, personally demanding exposure to settings vital for the social health of our society and to engender interest and commitment from fields that can potentially contribute to our understanding of these settings. *Undergraduates are no minuscule fraction of what we call the general public. They become parents, legislators, and members of boards of education. They vote on matters educational; their comprehension of these matters, generally speaking, is at best superficial and at worst unwittingly destructive.* The surprise would be if the situation were otherwise. What in their experience permits them to take distance from, to reexamine, to *reexperience* settings in which they spent years, to see these settings not as bounded, walled-off oases but as reflections of a distinctive society with its own history and traditions? What we call the liberal arts are fields of thought and inquiry explicitly intended to liberate students from a subjectivity and a parochialism in which the present blots out the past, ideas such as the world was born yesterday, what people created and did in the past are of no import for how we should think and act in a present from which a variety of futures are possible.

My proposal takes on significance only if you believe that the present state of our educational system has become the Achilles heel in our social body. If you so believe, it follows that our young people should no longer remain ignorant of the nature of this system, and that is what informs my proposal. I do not present it as a panacea, and it certainly is not in the category of quick fixes. We have had a surfeit of quick-fix proposals and a virtual absence of courses of action based on a long-term, prevention-oriented perspective. As I read history, among the truly potent factors that transform any societal institution are demographic changes with which are associated new attitudes, outlooks, values, and courses of action. That is why wars transform societies. That is why other national catastrophes—The Great Depression of the thirties, the current economic recession, racial strife, assassination of public figures—have differential effects on diverse groups, produce generational gaps and conflicts, and can influence such social barometers as birth rate, living styles, voting behavior, career choice, and more.

No reader of this book has to be persuaded that our schools are not understandable apart from demographic–cultural changes in the post–World War II era. Such changes have always been a feature of our schools. It used to be that the consequences of these changes would come into national awareness every 10 years or so, proposals for remediation of problems would be broadcast, followed relatively quickly by a pervasive amnesia. What is distinctive in the post–World War II era is that amnesia is no longer possible. Daily we are reminded that our educational system has to be changed and improved. Unfortunately, we are not also reminded that our past efforts at improvement have not worked and that those now being proposed are old wines in new bottles. We are not told that we have to adopt a long-term, preventive strategy. Even when that strategy is proclaimed in the abstract, one is left with the question: Where's the beef?

A local chain of clothing stores advertises, "An educated consumer is our best customer." That logo undergirds my proposal. To the extent that we seriously and meaningfully expose young college students to what we call education and schools, we stand a chance of getting more sophisticated consumers of public education.

My proposal will require an articulated national public policy affirming the importance of providing college students the opportunity to participate in the program I have sketched. It will also require affirmation of the importance of gaining the interest and commitment of the social science disciplines. This, I must emphasize, would not be the first time that the federal government, in the face of a national problem or crisis, has proclaimed a policy and received legislative approval explicitly intended to alter in some way the priorities of this or that part of our colleges and universities. Indeed, beginning with our entry into World War II, and with increasing frequency in the postwar decades, higher education has been transformed by public policies affecting the selection and support of students and faculty, and the creation of new programs and even fields.[3]

In regard to my proposal, the question will be this: Under what conditions and with what incentives would social science departments be willing to participate in such an undergraduate program? And by participate I do not mean token gestures, especially since schools and school systems have not been anywhere near the mainstream of these fields. We are faced with the chicken and egg problem in that my proposal requires changes in both students and faculty. I would argue that the quality of the program—the intellectual and personal fires it lights in students—will reflect the glow of the fires lit in faculty by what for them will be a new intellectual, hands-on experience. What that faculty can count on is the burning desire of young people who, surface appearances notwithstanding, long for experience that will be intellectually stimulating, engender a sense of personal growth, and enlarge their understanding of the world they live in. That, of course, is what faculty want for themselves. *And, I cannot refrain from adding, the faculty who become part of this new venture will soon find that what they want for themselves, and what they want their students to want, is what the bulk of children in our schools want but rarely experience.* That would be the beginning of wisdom and the spur to change. The more people who attain that wisdom, the more we stand a chance of seeing and acting on the difference between reform and prevention, between the short- and long-term perspective.

My proposal will cost money. I am not advocating that we get that money by reducing support for programs that, however they have the features of a Band-Aid, will in no way alter the incidence of problems. I am not an advocate for malign neglect. You do not walk away from these problems. In the best clinical tradition, you do the best you can on the basis of what you think will be helpful to problem children and schools. That our best has not been helpful, that what we think we know is riddled with unexamined and faulty assumptions, I have discussed in previous books. But I recognize and understand that when you are on the firing line, all the pressures are on you to act, to do something, even if that something is based largely on hope, prayer, and ignorance of similar past efforts. But to understand all is not to forgive all. At some point, those pressures to act *now* should not blind one to the obvious: Reform, even secondary prevention, is second best to primary prevention. If you accept that obvious fact, then you are required to focus on how educational personnel are attracted to, selected for, and prepared for

careers in education. My undergraduate proposal addresses those issues only
in part because its overarching goal is to broaden and deepen the perspectives of a crucial segment of our population who are currently or will be uneducated consumers of education.

And what is the mark? Our aim should be to prepare educators for the
realities of schools and school systems, and how they transact with the dynamics of other parts of our social system, and to do this in ways that instill in
educators a proactive rather than a reactive stance to change and innovation.
Such a stance is the polar opposite of an intellectual and professional passiv-
ity guaranteed to produce a sense of victimization, powerlessness, and resignation. You cannot be fully professional unless you have a secure basis for
"professing," for advocating, for acting, for having weapons for engaging in
the predictable battles about what schools are for, that is, who "owns" them,
and by what criteria outcomes and personnel should be judged.

Several decades ago, Kenneth Davidson, Burton Blatt, and I wrote a small
book entitled, *The Preparation of Teachers: An Unstudied Problem in Education*
(1962/1986). That book went out of print and mind very quickly. The central point was that the preparation of educators ill prepared people for the realities they would encounter in the "real world," and that gulf could and should
no longer be tolerated. Subsequent years have proved us right, a conclusion
some reviewers shared when a somewhat enlarged version of the book was
republished in 1989. Even so, in every sleep-producing report I have read
on school reform, the problem of preparation of educators has, for all practical purposes, been ignored. That I continue to pursue and agonize about
the problem may be viewed by some as manifestation of a pathological rep-
etition-compulsion on my part. To such a diagnosis I can only say that what
I advocate has rarely met with disagreement from educators on the firing
line. These educators are far more aware of the problem than any other group
with whom I have discussed the issues.

In 1903 John Dewey wrote an article "Democracy in Education," published in *The Elementary School Teacher.* (I am indebted to Ray Budde for
reminding me of that article, which was reprinted in *Progressive Education,*
1931, *8*(3), 216–218, and again in *Education Today* in 1940, a book edited
by Joseph Ratner.) That article should be read in its entirety. For my present
purposes it is sufficient to present a condensation of the article that Budde
sent me together with a copy of the original article. I am grateful for his permission to use his condensation.

> Until the public-school system is organized in such a way that every
> teacher has some regular and representative way in which he or she
> can register judgment upon matters of educational importance, with
> the assurance that this judgment will somehow affect the school sys-

tem, the assertion that the present system is not, from the internal standpoint, democratic seems to be justified.

What does democracy mean save that the individual is to have a share in determining the conditions and the aims of his own work and that on the whole, through the free and mutual harmonizing of different individuals, the work of the world is better done than when planned, arranged, and directed by a few, no matter how wise or of how good intent that few? How can we justify our belief in the democratic principle elsewhere, and then go back entirely upon it when we come to education?

If the teaching force is inept and unintelligent and irresponsible, surely the primary problem is that of their improvement. Only by sharing in some responsible task does there come a fitness to share in it. The argument that we must wait until men and women are fully ready to assume intellectual and social responsibilities would have defeated every step in the democratic direction that has ever been taken. The prevalence of methods of authority and of external dictation and direction tends automatically to perpetuate the very condition of inefficiency, lack of interest, inability to assume positions of self-determination, which constitute the reasons that are depended upon to justify the regime of authority.

All other reforms are conditioned upon reform in the quality and character of those who engage in the teaching profession. Just because education is the most personal, the most intimate, of all human affairs, there more than anywhere else, the sole ultimate reliance and final source of power are in the training, character, and intelligence of the individual. But as long as a school organization which is undemocratic in principle tends to repel from all but the higher portions of the school system those of independent force, of intellectual initiative, and of inventive ability, or tends to hamper them in their work after they find their way into the schoolroom, so long all other reforms are compromised at their source and postponed indefinitely for fruition.

Dewey was absolutely correct in describing what schools can do to teachers and others. Can we prepare educators to understand and cope better with the realities and organization of schools so that they can play a more proactive role in changing the existing scheme of things? Can we? We had better try. The stakes are higher than ever before. If, as Dewey said, we wait until we are certain about what will happen, we will prove that the more things change, the more they will remain the same. The quest for certainty (the title of one of Dewey's greatest books) is an invitation to defeat.

My proposal for all college undergraduates elicited no comment whatsoever in any of the reviews of the book even though those reviews were very favorable. Nor did any reviewer see (or comment on) the *connection* between the chapter from which the preceding comments were taken and the one that preceded it with the title "When Medical Education was Anti-Educational." That chapter was about the 1910 Flexner Report on Medical Education in the United States and Canada, a study and report that played a crucial role in transforming medical education. The point of that chapter was that Abraham Flexner exposed the semiscandalous, uncoordinated relationship (1) between the undergraduate and medical school years; (2) between what passed then for medical education and concomitant hands-on experience; and (3) the near total absence of mutual influence between theorists and researchers, on the one hand, and medical school faculty, on the other hand.[4] What Flexner envisioned was a medical school faculty with one foot in teaching and research and the other foot in the real world of caring for sick people. One of the reasons the chapter on Flexner preceded the one containing my undergraduate proposal had two parts. First, I wanted to indicate that the relationship between preparatory programs today—in regard to substance and faculty—and the real world of schools—needed rethinking and overhaul. Second, the gulf between departments or schools of education and the social sciences impoverished both and set drastic limits on what we could and needed to learn about our *system* of education and what that knowledge meant for action and change. Flexner's report had enormous, positive implications for undergraduate as well as medical education. My undergraduate proposal was a way by which I could make that point. In my mind, at least, the chapters were very much of a piece.

It is noteworthy that Flexner was not a physician. (His brother was an outstanding researcher–physician of his day.) Flexner was one of the two outstanding educators of the period. It is equally noteworthy that the Flexner study and report was commissioned by the Carnegie Foundation for the Advancement of *Teaching*. And it is not, therefore, surprising that for him two questions were uppermost in his mind. What *fields of inquiry* were essential for medical education and practice? How in medical education should theory, research, *teaching*, and practice be *organized*? And how can that organization rest on the values and processes of *continuous improvement*?

I said that Flexner was one of the two most outstanding educators of those times. The other one was John Dewey. It was Dewey who in his 1899 presidential address to the American Psychological Association, in a paper entitled, "Psychology and Social Practice," explicitly made the point that the field of education be seen as embedded in the social sciences. That point went nowhere in a higher education community in which specialization, turf, and status began to make a mockery of the phrase "a community of scholars." Each of the social sciences went its own way but education was not on any of those ways. Indeed, education was an arena the social sciences rather explicitly avoided. Colleges and universities are obvious stakeholders in and governors of the system of education. Any major reform effort that rivets primarily on public schools as if they do not function in a larger system of governance is missing the forest for the trees.

NOTES

[1]Lortie's 1975 book provided a long overdue, comprehensive, searching analysis of the nature and shortcomings of the preparation of teachers. Indeed, Lortie made plain that teaching lacked the major features of a profession, let alone a mature one. Although his work is regarded, and deservedly so, as a modern classic, it has not for all practical purposes impacted preparatory programs, a kind of instance of a prophet with honor but without acceptance on the level of appropriate action.

[2]The most recent example is a book *Who Will Teach? Policies That Matter* by Murnane, Singer, Willett, Kemple, and Olsen (1991). It is a book that analyzes the factors affecting teacher supply and comes up with conclusions disconfirming what is called the conventional wisdom. Murnane, the senior author, is an economist who before he did his graduate work in economics was a public school teacher. Still another example is a fascinating book by Pauly, *The Classroom Crucible* (1991), on the dynamics of power in the classroom.

Still another example is a 1984 paper by Henry Levin, an economist, on the seemingly universally held assumption that the amount of time that one is exposed to instruction or engaged in learning *must* bear some relation to what is learned. Levin demonstrates that the validity of that assumption depends on variables ignored by those who prefer simple but misleading assumptions. The wisdom in his paper has yet to be taken seriously.

[3]On November 12, 1991 C-Span was televising a discussion in the House of Representatives on a bill (H.R. 3508) intended to stimulate and support medical schools to develop programs for the preparation of physicians who would practice in underserved, rural, or inner-city areas. As several representatives said, medical schools value specialty training far more than training in primary care or family medicine, even though the need for primary care physicians becomes more pressing with each passing year. It is unlikely that very many medical schools will take advantage of the incentives the bill provides. Some will, and if their numbers will be fewer than the problem requires, we should be thankful for small favors. My undergraduate proposal would meet the same fate, assuming, of course, that the problem my proposal addresses ever gets recognized as a problem. Quite an assumption, I know. But my point here is not the degree of acceptance or the outcomes of such efforts but the fact that universities are subject to pressures for change and do change, however slowly or grudgingly. I venture the prediction that unless universities more quickly, more willingly, and more creatively change in regard to the preparation of medical and educational personnel, the time will come when they will be forced to change. At present, they have

options. If in the future they are forced to change, it will be another instance of substituting one set of intractable problems for another.

[4]Compared to the preparation of educators today, that of medical school students up until early in this century can legitimately be termed appalling. For example, it was possible in some states to enter a medical school without having gone to college. Many medical schools were not connected with a university, and many were not connected with hospitals!

A System That Does Not and Cannot Learn

It was not my intention to lay out in detail a plan for a new governance system for education. It was my intention to describe some of the features of a new system but even that was secondary to providing an answer to the question: What is the overarching purpose of schooling? No defender of any system of governance will deny that there is an overarching purpose, one that takes precedence over other purposes. That is to say, if that purpose is not being achieved, the system has failed. Purposes are not articulated and made public for the hell of it, they are intended to be taken seriously. In regard to education I have never met anyone who disagreed with the overarching purpose I have discussed in this book. And no one asserted that our schools, generally speaking, are achieving that purpose at all well. The assertions range from vehement condemnation to a plaintive "they never have done well and maybe that is in the nature of things," with most people in between on this continuum of dissatisfaction. What is instructive is that no one, when asked, went on to say that the governance system was the major culprit. They would say that the "system" was clearly the major factor, but they did not mean by system the different stakeholders in the system. To them the system is what is ordinarily meant by the schools in a particular district or community, i.e., buildings, a board of education, a superintendent, other administrators, teachers, and students. My intention in this book was to indicate how narrow that conception of system is because it obscures how the local "system" is embedded in a larger one in which stakeholders geographically distant influence and, directly or indirectly, drastically limit any effort to improve the local schools. Over the years we have learned a great deal about how governors of local schools are effective obstacles to change, not because they deliberately wish to be obstacles but because they govern to sustain law and order and uniformity. They do not govern in order to use the resources available to them to achieve an overarching purpose they publicly espouse. In fact, one of the most significant things we have learned is that it is inevitable that the gulf between what they espouse and what they do will be virtually unbridgeable. But that is also the case for other stakeholders in the larger system. This book was written because of my belated conviction that the larger system is unrescuable because it is not one that has taken the overarching purpose seriously, it cannot take it seriously, and there is no reason to believe that it can take it seriously in the future.

I say belatedly for three reasons. The first is that none of the major reform efforts have demonstrated that their very modest accomplishments here and there have spread beyond here and there. That is to say, the governance system is clearly and simply not geared to spread new ideas and practices through the system, i.e., beyond the sites where the reformers had demonstrated their very modest accomplishments. The second reason is that in each case these limited accomplishments required an heroic expenditure of time, energy, and money overcoming the resistance to change the current system virtually guarantees. If we have learned anything about the dynamics of resistance—in individuals and complicated organizations—it is the ease and subtlety with which the resistance shows up in new guises.

The third reason is that I was initially overwhelmed by my conviction because it confronted me with the "so what you do?" question. What plan did I have to offer? Scores of practical questions streamed through my mind. How should I deal with them in any proposed plan? It dawned on me that I was making the mistake of flying into action, so to speak. Assuming I could come up with a detailed plan, would that be the most productive first step? But I knew that I could not come up with such a plan. But what if I could? What was the likelihood that the details of the plan would become the object of critical scrutiny distracting the attention of its readers from the basic question: Do you truly believe that the overarching purpose of schooling is twofold—to recognize and respect individuality and to create and sustain contexts of productive learning? Is that for you rhetoric or a moral–educational imperative? Is your agreement with that purpose glib, or is it a purpose grounded in personal experience? Or is it, as in my case, that the purpose was an imperative but given the current system as well as the public's imprisonment in custom and tradition, what could I as a single individual do? Why spend time in my remaining years devising a detailed plan that required a thought-through conceptual and visceral understanding and acceptance of what we know about productive learning? Yes, I was obligated to give *some* features of a plan that would illustrate the implications for the purpose of governance. Those implications were what I wanted readers to recognize, just as I wanted them to confront the unrescuability of what we now have. Those implications are not now in currency, i.e., they are for all practical purposes not being discussed.

In several places in this book I refer to the movie *Mr. Holland's Opus*. Here I wish to note that I made a real effort to elicit reactions from two groups: my friends and educators with whom I came into contact. No one, but no one, said that what the movie depicted were unusual occurrences. One teacher summed up what all others said, "Insofar as student behavior and attitude is concerned, the picture is very realistic. In regard to those who ran the high schools it was right on target." What I found both surprising and dispiriting is that when I asked what lesson should be drawn from the film, the reply was basically that those who ran the school were by and large insensitive, obtuse personalities interested almost exclusively with sustaining mindless routines and practices. No one, including those who were educators, in any way indicated that what they saw indicted a governance that was not based on a respect for individuality or concern for productive learning. It was as if governance was a matter of personality.

It was what was missing in those reactions that told me that what I needed to do was not to develop a detailed plan for governance—a task no one person should be expected to confront or is able to do—but to rivet on the relationship between purpose and governance. *That* relationship needs to get into currency; it has to be seen as the crucial issue in matters of educational change. That realization allowed me to write this book and not to be intimidated by the criticism that the plan was too sketchy, that I provided no answers, no equivalent of a helpful road map, by which many practical problems would have to be handled. And I proceeded on the hope and belief that once the issue begins to gain currency the details of a plan will begin to emerge. At the present time the problem is not one whose time has come. When we say that the time has come for a practical problem to be dealt with forthrightly, it is because it has gained, slowly or quickly, a currency denoting public awareness. President Franklin Roosevelt entertained the desirability of a national health insurance program but decided against trying to enact one. President Truman articulated publicly the need for such a program but it fell on unreceptive ears. By playing the major role in passing the medicare legislation,

President Johnson gave currency to the idea of such a program. Every president after him was pressured to consider such a plan, testimony that the need for such a program had widespread currency. If we still do not have such a program despite the overwhelming desire for such a program, it is in large measure because we are far from agreement about the relationship between the purpose of the program and a system of governance for that purpose. But at least we are at the point where purpose is clear and there is legitimate concern that we not devise a governance system that will subvert that purpose, although the nonnational insurance programs being implemented on a large scale are being criticized for having a governance structure that cannot serve the purpose of efficient, humane medical care because their main purpose is to be profitable. The reader has undoubtedly heard a variant of the joke of three physicians seeking entrance into heaven. The first doctor, a surgeon, recounts in great detail and with numbers the lives he has saved; he is told he may enter. The second physician, a family practitioner, describes how he was responsive night and day to his patients, even traveling distances in rain and snow storms to render care. He is told he can enter. The third physician says that he created and ran an HMO that served thousands of people who received quality but cost-effective medical care. He was told he could enter heaven but he could only stay for 2 nights and 3 days.

All of the preceding is by way of saying that I understand if the reader who truly accepts the overarching purpose is overwhelmed by the "what do I—we do?" question. In my case I did what I do best, which is not to say I do it all that well. I wrote a book, *Letters to a Serious Educational President* (1993b), in which I urge the first president of the 21st century to convene a convention devoted to educational purpose and governance. I had said similar things in others of my recent books. I have hectored foundation people. I assail audiences with the same message. I do what I can to bring the problem to people's attention. Each reader, those who agree with me, has to take advantage of whatever opportunities are afforded her or him to contribute to increasing the currency of the issues. And all of this at a time when there is no credible evidence whatsoever that improvement of our schools is even a blip on the horizon. Beginning in 1965 I began to predict that our schools were going to decline in quality and outcomes, especially our urban schools. I had spent enough time in enough classrooms and schools, and I was aware of the social change that became obvious in the sixties, to see the obvious: Schools were places for unproductive learning. If it was obvious, it was not forceful enough to direct my attention to the system *qua* system, which I unreflectively believed was amenable to change. As time went on I concluded otherwise.

The gulf between urban and nonurban schools grows larger each year, far larger than test scores indicate if you take attitude and motivation into account. I cannot predict how and how fast the destabilizing consequences of the gulf will become so clear and so frightening as to require us, finally, to recognize that what we have must be scrapped. If in the years to come the purpose–governance relationship does not get the currency it should, we shall pay a price in human and fiscal terms that will be truly staggering.

I know I sound like a prophet of doom and gloom. That is precisely what I was called more than three decades ago when I said the educational reform movement would fail to have generalizing, positive effects. I have had no reason to change my mind. This in no way should be interpreted as suggesting that we stop doing what we are doing in our heres and theres to improve the quality of our schools. Even though Mr. Holland's program and employment were terminated, he and others knew that he had positively affected the lives of students. *That is no small feat.* There are more than a few Mr. Hollands whose accomplishments are real and unrecognized. And that is one of the major points in this book: We have a system that cannot learn and that suffuses that learning beyond the narrow confines of this or that classroom or this or that school. When Mr. Holland left his school, it was no different than when he had started to teach there. My bleak outlook is not about the potentialities of educators who are victims of the system but about the lack of a discussion centering on the dysfunction between purpose and governance.

References

Alinsky, S. (1992). *Let them call me rebel*. New York: Vintage.

Arnstine, D. (1995). *Democracy and the arts of schooling*. Albany, NY: State University Press of New York.

Barker, R.G., & Gump, P.V. (1964). *Big school, small school*. Stanford, CA: Stanford University Press.

Butterworth, B., & Weinstein, R.S. (July, 1997). Enhancing motivation and opportunity in elementary school: A case study of principal leadership. *Elementary School Journal, 97,* 57–80.

Conant, J.B. (1963). *The education of teachers*. New York: McGraw-Hill.

Cowen, E., et al. (1996). *School based prevention for at risk children. The Primary Mental Health Project*. Washington, DC: American Psychological Association.

Cross City Campaign for Urban School Reform. (May, 1995). *Reinventing central office. A primer for successful schools*. 407 S. Dearborn Street, Suite 1725, Chicago, IL 60605.

Dewey, J. (1899). *School and society*. Chicago: University of Chicago Press.

Dewey, J. (1916). *Democracy and education*. New York: Macmillan.

Dewey, J. (1931). Democracy in education. *Progressive Education, 8*(3), 216–218.

Dewey, J. (1933). *How we think*. Boston: D.C. Heath.

Dewey, J. (1934). *Art as experience*. New York: Minton, Balch.

Flexner, A. (1960). *Medical education in the United States and Canada*. Washington, D.C.: The Carnegie Foundation for the Advancement of Teaching. (Originally published in 1910)

Forester, A.D. (October, 1991a). *An Examination of Parallels Between Deming's Model for Transforming Industry and Current Trends in Education*. Paper presented at the National Learning Foundation's TQE/TQM seminar, Washington, D.C.

Forester, A.D., & Reinhard, M. (February, 1991b). *On the move—Teaching the learners' way in grades 4–7*. Winnipeg, Canada: Pequis Publishers.

Glasser, W. (1990). The quality school: What motivates the ants? *Phi Delta Kappan,* 424–435.

Heckman, P., et al. (1995). *The courage to change: Stories from successful school reform.* Newbury Park, CA: Corwin Press.

Horwitt, S.D. (1992). *Let them call me rebel. Saul Alinsky: His life and Legacy.* New York: Vintage Books.

Industrial Areas Foundation. (1992). *IAF. Fifty Years of Change.* IAF, 36 New Hyde Park Road, Franklin Square, NY 11010.

Lieberman, A. (Ed.). (1995). *The work of restructuring schools.* New York: Teachers College Press.

Lieberman, A., & Miller, L. (1990). *The world and work of teachers.* New York: Teachers College Press.

Longo, P. (1979). *Program Evaluation: Project City Science.* New York: Queens College, Department of Education.

Lortie, D. (1975). *School teacher.* Chicago: University of Chicago Press.

Monterra, V. (1996). *Bridging the gap: A case study of the home–school–community relationship at Ochoa Elementary School.* Doctoral dissertation, College of Education, University of Arizona (Tucson).

Murnane, R., et al. (1991). *Who will teach? Policies that matter.* Cambridge, MA: Harvard University Press.

O'Connor, E. (1956). *The last hurrah.* New York: Bantam Press.

Pauly, E. (1991). *The classroom crucible. What really works.* New York: Basic Books.

Ravitch, D. (Autumn, 1995). Adventures in wonderland. *American Scholar.*

Rogers, M.B. (1990). *Cold anger.* Denton, Texas: University of North Texas Press.

Sarason, S.B. (1972). *The creation of settings and the future societies.* San Francisco: Jossey-Bass.

Sarason, S.B. (1983). *Schooling in America: Scapegoat and salvation.* New York: Free Press.

Sarason, S.B. (1990a). *The predictable failure of educational reform.* San Francisco: Jossey-Bass.

Sarason, S.B. (1990b). *The challenge of art to psychology.* New Haven: Yale University Press.

Sarason, S.B. (1992). *The case for change. Rethinking the preparation of educators.* San Francisco: Jossey-Bass.

Sarason, S.B. (1993a). *You are thinking of teaching? Opportunities, problems, realities.* San Francisco: Jossey-Bass.

Sarason, S.B. (1993b). *Letters to a serious educational president.* Newbury Park, CA: Corwin Press.

Sarason, S.B. (1995a). *School change. The personal development of a point of view.* New York: Teachers College Press.

Sarason, S.B. (1995b). *Parental involvement and the political principle. Why the existing governance structure of schools should be abolished.* San Francisco: Jossey-Bass.

Sarason, S.B. (1996a). *Barometers of social change.* San Francisco: Jossey-Bass.

Sarason, S.B. (1996b). *Revisiting the culture of the school and the problem of change.* New York: Teachers College Press. (Originally published in 1971, 2nd ed., 1982)

Sarason, S.B., Carroll, C., Maton, K., Cohen, S., & Lorentz, E. (1986). *Human services and resource networks.* Cambridge, MA: Brookline Books. (Originally published by Jossey-Bass in 1977)

Sarason, S.B., Davidson, K., & Blatt, B. (1986). *The preparation of teachers: An unstudied problem in education.* Cambridge, MA: Brookline Books.

Sarason, S.B., & Lorentz, E. (1986). *The challenge of the resource exchange network.* Cambridge, MA: Brookline Books. (Originally published by Jossey-Bass in 1979)

Sarason, S.B., & Lorentz, E. (1997). *Coordination: Process, problems, and opportunities. In schools, private sector, and federal government.* San Francisco: Jossey-Bass.

Shanker, A. (1996, January 28). *Mr. Holland's Opus. New York Times* [Sunday: Review of the Week section].

Sharan, S. (Ed.). (1994). *Handbook of cooperative learning methods.* Westport, CT: Greenwood Press.

Sharan, S., Russell, P., Bergerance, Y., Hertz-Lazarowitz, R., & Brosh, T. (1982). *Cooperative learning, whole-class instruction, and the academic achievement and social relations of pupils in ethnically mixed junior high schools.* Final report to Ford Foundation on Israel Ministry of Education and Culture.

Sharan, S., & Sharan, Y. (1992). *Expanding cooperative through group investigation.* New York: Teachers College Press.

Stake, R. (1996). *Strategies: teacher professional development in Chicago school reform.* University of Illinois, Urbana: Center for Instructional Research and Curriculum Evaluation.

Steinberg, L. (September 13, 1996). Do mom and dad deserve an F in education? *Forward,* p. 21. (English edition)

Steinberg, L., Brown, B., & Dornbusch, S. (1996). *Beyond the classroom.* New York: Simon and Shuster.

Trubowitz, S., & Longo, P. (1997). *How it works: Inside a school/college collaboration.* New York: Teachers College Press.

Trubowitz, S., et al. (1984). *When a college and a school work together.* Boston: Institute for Responsive Education.

Vlahakis, R., & the Students of Shoreham-Wading River School. (1978). *Kids who care.* Oakdale, NY: Dowling College Press.

Watriss, W. (November 22, 1990). Interview with Virginia Ramirez and Javier Parra. *Texas Observer.*

Wertheimer, M. (1945). *Productive thinking.* New York: Harper.

Wilson, K. (May, 1994). Wisdom centered learning: Striking a new paradigm for education. *School Administrator, 51*(5), 26.

Wilson, K., & Daviss, B. (1996). *Redesigning education.* New York: Teachers College Press. (Originally published in 1994 by Holt)

About the Author

SEYMOUR B. SARASON is professor of psychology emeritus in the Department of Psychology and at the Institution for Social and Policy Studies of Yale University. In 1962 he founded and directed the Yale Psycho-Educational Clinic, one of the first research and training sites in community psychology. Fields in which he has made special contributions include mental retardation, culture and per-sonality, projective techniques, teacher training, anxiety in children, and school reform. His numerous books and articles reflect his broad interests.

Dr. Sarason received his Ph.D. degree from Clark University in 1942 and holds honorary doctorates from Syracuse University, Queens College, Rhode Island College, and Lewis and Clark College. He has received awards from the American Association on Mental Deficiency and the American Psychological Association, which presented him with the Lifetime Achievement Award in 1996.